The Path
of the Ocean

The Path of the Ocean

TRADITIONAL POETRY OF POLYNESIA

collected and edited by
MARJORIE SINCLAIR

University of Hawaii Press
Honolulu

Copyright © 1982 by Marjorie Sinclair
All Rights Reserved
Copyright acknowledgments appear in the list of sources
beginning on page 209.
Manufactured in the United States of America

Library of Congress Cataloging in Publication Data
Main entry under title:

The Path of the ocean.

　Bibliography: p.
　1. Folk poetry, Polynesian—Translations into
English.　2. Folk poetry, English—Translations from
Polynesian language.　I. Sinclair, Marjorie Jane Putnam.
II. Title.
PL6408.65.E5　1982　　398.2'0996　　82-8611
ISBN 0-8248-0804-5　　　　　　　　AACR2

For Leon

*I knew
the language of the fishbone,
the tooth of the hard fish,
chill of the latitudes,
blood of the coral, the silent
night of the whale,
for from land to land I went.*
                    Pablo Neruda

*Les migrations plus énormes que les
anciennes invasions.*
                    Rimbaud

Contents

Preface xv
Introduction xvii

HAWAII
From "An ancient prayer" 3
From "The Kumulipo" 4
The water of Kane 13
An appeal for rain 15
Prayer to Kane 16
Harvest prayer 17
House dedication prayer 18
Tree-felling song 19
Pele and Hi'i-aka 20
  The coming of Pele 20
  The spy 22
  Watch your way 23
  Songs of the girl without hands 24
  Stormy weather 25
  Kauhi 26
  Hi'i-aka's song at Ka-'ena 27
  Hi'i-aka's song for the Stone of Kaua'i 29
  Songs to the ghost of Lohi'au 30
  Hi'i-aka chants to restore Lohi'au to life 31
  Vision of the burning 32
  A storm, a rough surf 33
  The fires of Pele 34
  Lohi'au's song 35
From "Fallen is the chief" 36
From "A chant for the island of Maui" 38
A kapu is placed 40

Love song   42
The salt pond of Mana   43
From "Ka-'ahu-manu's dirge for
   Ke'e-au-moku"   44
From "Birth chant for Kau-i-ke-ao-uli"   45
A name song for Princess Nahi'ena'ena   48
Song   49
Shark song   50
Chant composed while drunk   51
Lament on the death of a first child   52
From "A name chant for Kupake'e"   53
Song of the chanter Ka-'ehu   54
Piano at evening   56

SAMOA
From a creation chant   59
Chant for the whale   60
Lovers' farewell   61

TONGA
The weather shore of Vavau   65
Love song   67
How I love her way   68
Poem of Falepapalangi to Mamaeaepoto   70
Poem of Veehala   73

THE SOCIETY ISLANDS
Creation chant   77
Chant for a royal birth   79
Anointing the royal child   80
Chant to usher in the dawn   81
The song of Ru's sister   82
Warrior's taunting song   83
Song of Pa'ea   84
Invocation for fire-walking   85

A chief's refusal 86
A chief's lament for home 87

THE TUAMOTUS
Creation chant 91
Greeting of Tane 92
Farewell to my land 93
Rata's lament for his father 94
Chant to announce a catch of turtle 95
Prayer offering turtle flesh to the gods 96
Prayer for arrival of turtle at the temple 97
Chant for Horahora 98
Chant of Kororupo 100

THE MARQUESAS
Chant honoring a first-born son 103
Love song 104
Be careful 106
Hiva'oa balances 107
The faufe'e bird 108
Strong fires disturb 109
When a man's body is young 110

EASTER ISLAND
A chant of creation 113
A prayer for rain 115
Dampened by dew 116
Love song 117
You are sick with love 118
O Manu 119

MANGAREVA
Tahaki's drum 123
Song of departure 125
The message of the frigate bird 126

The rich and the poor   128
The flower at the spring   130
Joy turns to sadness   131
Sea burial of Toga's daughter   132
The sacred house   133
The casting out of love   134
I am left alone   135
Lament   136
The canoe of Mamau-ora   137
Haul away   138
Song of things in the upper world   139
Lament for old age   141

COOK ISLANDS
    Prayer over a human sacrifice to Rongo   145
    Where has she gone   147
    Puvai leading a band of ghosts to the
        underworld   148
    Death lament for Varenga   150

TUVALU
    Vaitupu songs   155

KAPINGAMARANGI
    The post standing in the sky   159
    Love song   160
    I go down to the lagoon   161
    I am on the water   162
    Chant for the bonito canoe   163
    Search for   164
    The man stayed   165

TIKOPIA
    Lament for a friend   169
    Dream song   170

NEW ZEALAND

    Creation chant   173
    Creation chant   175
    Creation chant   176
    The creation of woman   178
    Chant for bailing a canoe   179
    Arrival at New Zealand   181
    From a lament for a son who burned
        to death   182
    Prayer for victory in battle   185
    Chant to incite warriors   186
    A war chant   187
    Spiders, hide my face   188
    Te Rauparaha's farewell to Kawhia   189
    Potatau's song of sorrow   191
    Dirge for a chief   192
    A ritual spell   193
    Vision   194
    Song of mourning   195
    A charm: Is it the wind?   196
    Song of a second wife   197
    The deserted girl's lament   198
    A mourning song for Rangiahao   199
    A song of sickness   200
    Chant to restore breath to a dead person   201
    A lament for his house   202
    How the trembling shakes me   204
    Oh! I am torn with fear   205
    On the hilltops   206
    Love song   207
    An ancient flute song   208

Sources   209

Preface

THIS ANTHOLOGY of traditional Polynesian poetry was selected from translations made by missionaries, travelers, anthropologists, ethnologists, informed amateurs and a few persons with literary interest. Consequently the use of language has great variety. Some translators had a sensitive awareness of how English might render the meaning of the original text. Others were primarily eager to get down meanings. Most were concerned with the material as a record, an artifact or an account of societal and religious patterns and customs—not as poetry. My concern has been to present this anthology as a volume of poetry.

The language used by some translators presents difficulties. One is poetic inversion of syntax and another the use of archaic diction. In the anthology I have made certain small alterations—I have changed words, punctuation or syntax, and have rephrased lines when necessary. I have removed poetic archaisms and affectations. The diacritical marks, however, are those used by the translators. In the Hawaiian Pele and Hiʻi-aka series I have retranslated several poems, using Nathaniel Emerson's work as a basis.

That these poems should be accompanied by some ethnological data is inevitable. I have limited myself to that which seemed necessary to make the poems as clear as possible. Persons who wish to pursue the ethnology can refer to the books and journals from which the material was taken. Such information will be found in the list of sources at the back.

I am very grateful to the following for their continued help in the work on this volume: to Renée Heyum, curator of the Pacific Collection at Hamilton Library, University of Hawaii, for invaluable advice about discovering sources, to Leon Edel and Galway Kinnell for a careful reading of the manuscript, and to W. S. Merwin for his reflections on poetry in translation. My primary debt is to the translators. I am also indebted to all those who through the years have guided and advised me in my pursuit of Polynesian poetry—Janet Bell, Alfons Korn, Katharine Luomala and Mary Kawena Pukui.

Introduction

THE POEMS in this anthology were composed by a race of seafarers and island dwellers who crossed thousands of miles of ocean in frail vessels, guiding themselves by the stars and the feel of wave and wind. The poems reflect the ways in which they saw their universe of sea and sky and the scattered fragments of land they found and settled. Their chants tell of gods and rituals of gods, of heroes and heroisms—as well as the particulars of ordinary life. They sing of primary experience charged with emotion—birth, love, endurance, strife, death. Poetry was central to these people.

The islands of Polynesia fit neatly into a triangle with Hawaii at the north tip, New Zealand at the south and Easter Island at the east. The ocean area is vast, the land area small. There are tiny islands—atolls with mirroring lagoons; and large islands with mountains, volcanoes and even glaciers. Most of the islands are warm, usually comfortably warm; but there are more temperate climates as in New Zealand. The ancient voyagers found fair places to live.

Where did the Polynesians come from? They have a name for it: Hawaiki. The poets sing of a green and cherished place, a legendary homeland. Hawaii is named after it. Perhaps it is a place outside of Polynesia—the land from which they started. More likely it signifies an island or cluster of islands within the broad reaches of Polynesia itself.

There have been many theories about the original homeland of the Polynesians—that it was India, or

Indonesia or South America. A recent and widely accepted hypothesis suggests that a people, not yet Polynesian, started from the coastlands of Southeast Asia about the second millenium B.C. They moved slowly into and through the Philippines, through Melanesia and then out across the broad stretches of the sea toward the Polynesian Triangle. They reached the western tip about 1,000 B.C. Some recent research suggests an even earlier date. They settled in Samoa and Tonga, and they pushed eastward in long voyages. No other people journeyed so far—and in such small vessels—across thousands of miles of sea. They found and settled the Cook Islands, the Society Islands, the Marquesas, the Tuamotus. They drove north to Hawaii and south to New Zealand.

Was this voyaging caused by human discord, human need? Warfare, overpopulation? The threat of starvation? Perhaps. We can only surmise; no absolute answers are available. There may have been among some people an inner restlessness to escape from island limits, a constant reaching toward sea horizons. Did they consciously set out to find new islands? Or were the journeys of discovery largely accidental—canoes blown off course into unknown seaways? What we know is that the Polynesians sailed resolutely east and north and south from their first settlements at the western edge of the Polynesian Triangle. They even found that remote "Navel of the World," as the residents call it, Easter Island. The Polynesian dispersion and settlement are unusual in the history of the world, more like a flight of birds than an advance across the earth.

The Polynesians discovered and occupied the last uninhabited land area of the world, if we exclude the ice and snow of the polar regions. The area was composed of island groups, usually far distant from each other. On these islands of beauty and isolation, they established their distinctive culture and a literature of subtlety and resonance.

When did the poetry and storytelling begin? Again we can only guess. Man starts very early to put his feelings into words. And words become patterns of rhythm. The literature which we identify as Polynesian was composed after those early people began settling in the western part of the Triangle and then traveled eastward. In this process of dispersion they were already creating their culture. Stories and chants among all the islands tell of the same gods and goddesses, the same heroes and tricksters, the same great voyagers; even the cosmogonies are similar. Language and song traveled in the canoes with coconuts, taro, children and dogs. As the language traveled, it acquired many variations and transliterations. Aloha is elsewhere *talofa* or *aroha*. The god Kanaloa in Hawaii is Tangaloa or Tangaroa in other islands.

Life was easier in the Polynesian Triangle than in the earlier stopping places of those voyaging peoples. Douglas Oliver points out that the concern for material things which was present in Melanesia declined as they settled on milder islands. The Polynesians poured their energies, he says, "into elaborating their mythologies, their religious rites, and their political interrelationships"; and into composing and memorizing lengthy genealogies which sometimes commenced with a beautiful cosmogonic poem. While they were elaborating their mythologies, they also extended their legends and folktales, often into long cycles. They recounted their history, delivered splendid orations, composed charms and riddles. They sang of universal things—warfare, love and hate, the melancholy of growing old, birth and death, the beauty of rain, wind and sea.

In this process they developed their racial memory: they not only carried in themselves and transmitted to their children stories, myths and rituals, but trained themselves to remember long poems—the exact word orders, place names and allusions—even as the great epics were remembered in the west until the time came when they could be written down.

The Polynesian poet was trained in a formal school or by a master bard. When a student entered a course of instruction in poetry, chanting, music, dancing, he also entered a strictly patterned and austere way of life. His days were concentrated on learning—memory training—and perfecting his skills. In addition to chanting and dancing, many schools taught genealogies, myth and legend, temple ritual, the art of narrative, the art of oratory and astronomy. They trained troupes of chanters and dancers for both religious and secular purposes. The kind of training varied from island group to island group.

In the Marquesas, a father who wanted his son or daughter to be educated built a special house for a school and brought a bard to live in residence. The students were generally over twenty—they had to be serious and mature. Poetry, with music, dance and sacred lore, was a vital part of the pattern of society and as such could not be left to immature impulses. The bard himself had to exercise and maintain his skills and techniques. To prove that he was not in decline he often engaged in contests with other bards. In Mangareva there were experts, always of noble birth, called *rogorogo*. They had the role of historian, reciting genealogies, composing and singing chants which praised the aristocracy. The *rogorogo* were also

Introduction

educators; from their teachings the song composers took themes for their poems. The Society Islands were famous for the Ariori, a complex and powerful organization which trained large troupes of dancers and singers and staged elaborate theatrical performances and pageants. Some troupes performed at parties and celebrations and others in the temple. At their height, the Ariori traveled in great fleets of canoes among the islands and put on elaborate and glittering programs—a living archive of music, chants, poetry and drama.

Of all the unwritten poetry which has been translated from Polynesian materials, the Hawaiian Pele and Hiʻi-aka myth comes closest to epic scope and purpose. The poems were stored in the memories of many men and women and were widely scattered. They were collected in a volume of translations by Nathaniel B. Emerson, and I have included a selection in this anthology. It was Emerson's opinion that the Pele and Hiʻi-aka story "stands at the fountainhead of Hawaiian myth and is the matrix from which the unwritten literature of Hawaii drew its lifeblood." The collection of poems is rooted in the primal elements of nature in Hawaii, especially the volcanoes and their raging fires. The psychology of the characters reflects all the passions—love, hate, jealousy, anger, tenderness. Pele and Hiʻi-aka are goddesses. Lohiʻau is a mortal. The goddesses, like those of the Greeks, possess the human passions. Their drama is played out against the background of the Hawaiian chain in such fashion that the islands themselves become characters in the story.

In the Pele and Hiʻi-aka poems, places and their names are continually invoked—they serve as a source of power and imagination. The power of place holds true in all of Polynesia. The many place names in Polynesian poems suggest a constant, minute and often intense observation of nature. When translated, the place name is usually descriptive—often a single feature of a beautiful or beloved spot. This feature can become symbolic. It may be identified with human experience. It may recall a person or an event. More profoundly, the place name reminds a Polynesian of his origin and bond with earth and sea. A name can also summon up a legend or a myth—or wondrous things that have happened in a given locality. The imagination seizes the word. It may reveal romantic or melancholy feelings about rain: the cold rain of Waimea or the rain which "sounds" like lehua flowers. It may summon up a wind: the dust-scattering wind of Ka'u. The place name can be used for allusion, indirection and double meaning.

Such devices are important in Polynesian poetry. The Hawaiians have a word, *kaona,* for hidden meaning. Mary Kawena Pukui says of Hawaiian poetry that it has two meanings, the literal and the *kaona.* There are, however, some poems without the *kaona.* An illustration of the complexity of indirection is recorded in Thomas Barthel's *The Eighth Land.* He presents two versions of a translation of a birth chant for a royal child on Easter Island. He calls the first version the "exoteric" or public; he calls the second the "esoteric." He also suggests that there is a third level of interpretation possible, the erotic. His translation of the exoteric reads:

May the shadow of the king arise!
The feathered staffs do not (yet) call.
The many spears do not (yet) call.

> One has been invested who rises and does not (yet)
>   call.
> One has been invested with supernatural powers
>   who does not (yet) call.
> The black shadow is yours, oh king!
> The red shadow be yours, oh king!
> The white shadow be yours, oh king!

Barthel admits the difficulty and tentativeness of presenting the esoteric. But he gives the following translation as example.

> The king has been born!
> Bare of all coverings is he who is lofty as a rainbow.
> Like the red rays of the sun the god king triumphs!
> Arrived has the successor, lofty as a rainbow;
> Arrived has the one full of *mana*, the lofty
>   triumphs.
> Just now you have been born, oh king!
> You shall grow, oh king!
> You shall become great, oh king!

That one scholar could produce two such drastically different versions of the same poem illustrates the enormity of the problem of translating a literature so different from our own.

A great deal of work remains to be done with Polynesian poetry: more translations of untranslated work, new translations of what has already been done, and a continuing literary study of the poetry itself. Up to now, the translators have primarily been interested in recording history, material culture, social organization, religion, etc. Now we need to have translators who will treat the poems as works of literature, bringing to bear the penetration of literary scholarship. We also need translators who are poets. Polynesian poetry can become a tradition within which the contemporary Polynesian can work as he composes poetry today.

The arrangement of this anthology does not attempt to follow a historical or ethnographic scheme; it is, however, roughly geographic. I begin with Hawaii and travel southward, sometimes to the east and sometimes to the west until finally New Zealand is reached. The structure of the anthology is in reality a metaphor, a north to south journey. This is reflected in the title: *The Path of the Ocean*.

The dates or periods of these poems are conjectural —just as the chronology of Polynesian history is open to continual inquiry. One cannot know how long many of the poems have lived in the memory of the people. Some scholars have attributed certain poems to the eighteenth century—the Hawaiian "Kumulipo" is believed to have been composed in that century. There are many poems which perhaps should be dated much earlier. If specific poets are named, an approximate time can be suggested. Where missionary or other western influence is observed—as in the sound of a piano, the name of a ship, an image which seems to come from the Bible—it is obvious that the poem was composed after the arrival of Captain Cook. Another clue is the period in which the poem was collected in the field; on occasion the anthropologist knew the poet who had composed the poem. In the nineteenth century, Hawaiian-language newspapers gathered and published poems and chants and in this way preserved some of the unwritten literature. It will probably never be possible to give Polynesian poems a chronology in any western sense, for as we know the great library for this literature has been the human memory.

Notes

For the origin of the Polynesians: Robert C. Suggs, *The Island Civilizations of Polynesia* (Mentor Books, New York).

Douglas Oliver, *The Pacific Islands* (Doubleday Anchor Books, rev. ed., New York, 1961).

For the education of the poet: Teuira Henry, *Ancient Tahiti* (Bishop Museum Bulletin 48, Honolulu, 1928); Katharine Luomala, *Voices on the Wind* (Bishop Museum Press, Honolulu, 1955); Peter Buck, *Ethnology of Mangareva* (Bishop Museum Bulletin 157, Honolulu, 1938).

Nathaniel B. Emerson, *Pele and Hi'i-aka* (Honolulu, 1915).

Thomas Barthel, *The Eighth Land* (University Press of Hawaii, Honolulu, 1978).

Hawaii

From "An ancient prayer"

Lono is the god of harvest and agriculture.

The spirit is within the smooth bones of the god.
Here are the sacred signs of the assembly of Lono:
The voice of thunder bursts forth;
The rays of lightning flash;
The earthquake shakes the land;
The smoky cloud and the rainbow appear;
Heavy rain and high wind blow;
Whirlwinds sweep beneath the earth;
Rocks fall on stream banks;
Red mountain-streams rush to the sea.
Here are the water spouts;
The cluster clouds of heaven tremble;
Springs in the cliffs gush forth.
. . .
Here is Lono the bone of glory;
The bone placed in the clear sky.

From "The Kumulipo"

"The Kumulipo" is a genealogical prayer chant of more than two thousand lines. This kind of chant celebrates the nobility of a chief's family and connects it with the origin of things. The name, Kumulipo, means "beginning in deep darkness." The poem is divided into sixteen sections called *wa*. The earlier part, from which these selections are taken, belongs to the period called *Po*, the night. The second part belongs to *Ao*, the day. More than half the chant is composed of straight genealogical pairings.

Queen Liliuokalani dates the poem 1700 and writes that Keaulumoku composed it.

Birth of sea and land life

At the time when the earth became hot
At the time when the heavens turned about
At the time when the sun was darkened
To cause the moon to shine
The time of the rise of the Pleiades
The slime, this was the source of the earth
The source of the darkness that made darkness
The source of the night that made night
The intense darkness, the deep darkness
Darkness of the sun, darkness of the night
    Nothing but night.

The night gave birth
Born was Kumulipo in the night, a male
Born was Po'ele in the night, a female
Born was the coral polyp, born was the coral,
    came forth

Born was the grub that digs and heaps up the earth,
   came forth
Born was his child an earthworm, came forth
Born was the starfish, his child the small starfish
   came forth
Born was the sea cucumber, his child the small sea
   cucumber came forth
Born was the sea urchin, the sea urchin tribe
Born was the short-spiked sea urchin, came forth
Born was the smooth sea urchin, his child the long-
   spiked came forth
Born was the ring-shaped sea urchin, his child the
   thin-spiked came forth
Born was the barnacle, his child the pearl oyster
   came forth
Born was the mother-of-pearl, his child the oyster
   came forth
Born was the mussel, his child the hermit crab
   came forth
Born was the big limpet, his child the small limpet
   came forth
Born was the cowry, his child the small cowry
   came forth
Born was the naka shellfish, the rock oyster his
   child came forth
Born was the drupa shellfish, his child the bitter
   white shellfish came forth
Born was the conch shell, his child the small conch
   shell came forth
Born was the nerita shellfish, the sand-burrowing
   shellfish his child came forth
Born was the freshwater shellfish, his child the
   small freshwater shellfish came forth

Born was man for the narrow stream, the woman
	for the broad stream
Born was the Ekaha moss living in the sea
Guarded by the Ekahakaha fern living on land
Darkness slips into light
Earth and water are the food of the plant
The god enters, man cannot enter
Man for the narrow stream, woman for the
	broad stream
Born was the tough seagrass living in the sea
Guarded by the tough landgrass living on land
	REFRAIN
Man for the narrow stream, woman for the
	broad stream
Born was the 'A'ala moss living in the sea
Guarded by the 'Ala'ala mint living on land
	REFRAIN
Man for the narrow stream, woman for the
	broad stream
Born was the Manauea moss living in the sea
Guarded by the Manauea taro living on land
	REFRAIN
Man for the narrow stream, woman for the
	broad stream
Born was the Ko'ele seaweed living in the sea
Guarded by the long-jointed sugarcane, the
	ko'ele'ele, living on land
	REFRAIN
Man for the narrow stream, woman for the
	broad stream
Born was the Puaki seaweed living in the sea
Guarded by the Akiaki rush living on land

REFRAIN
Man for the narrow stream, woman for the
   broad stream
Born was the Kakalamoa living in the sea
Guarded by the moamoa plant living on land
REFRAIN
Man for the narrow stream, woman for the
   broad stream
Born was the Kele seaweed living in the sea
Guarded by the Ekele plant living on land
REFRAIN
Man for the narrow stream, woman for the
   broad stream
Born was the Kala seaweed living in the sea
Guarded by the 'Akala vine living on land
REFRAIN
Man for the narrow stream, woman for the
   broad stream
Born was the Lipu'upu'u living in the sea
Guarded by the Lipu'u living on land
REFRAIN
Man for the narrow stream, woman for the
   broad stream
Born was the Long-one living at sea
Guarded by the Long-torch living on land
REFRAIN
Man for the narrow stream, woman for the
   broad stream
Born was the Ne seaweed living in the sea
Guarded by the Neneleau living on land

REFRAIN
Man for the narrow stream, woman for the
    broad stream
Born was the hairy seaweed living in the sea
Guarded by the hairy pandanus vine living
    on land
Darkness slips into light
Earth and water are the food of the plant
The god enters, man cannot enter

The man with the water gourd, he is a god
Water that causes the withered vine to flourish
Causes the plant top to develop freely
Multiplying in the passing time
The long night slips along
Fruitful, very fruitful
Spreading here, spreading there
Spreading this way, spreading that way
Propping up earth, holding up the sky
The time passes, this night of Kumulipo
    Still it is night

Winged life

A male this, the female that
A male born in the time of black darkness
The female born in the time of groping in the
    darkness
Overshadowed was the sea, overshadowed the land
Overshadowed the streams, overshadowed the
    mountains
Overshadowed the dimly brightening night
The rootstalk grew forming nine leaves

Upright it grew with dark leaves
The sprout that shot forth leaves of high chiefs
Born was Poʻeleʻele the male
Lived with Pohaha a female
The rootstalk sprouted
    The taro stalk grew

Born was the Wood borer, a parent
Out came its child a flying thing, and flew
Born was the Caterpillar, the parent
Out came its child a Moth, and flew
Born was the Ant, the parent
Out came its child a Dragonfly, and flew
Born was the Grub, the parent
Out came its child the Grasshopper, and flew
Born was the Pinworm, the parent
Out came its child a Fly, and flew
Born was the egg, the parent
Out came its child a bird, and flew
Born was the Snipe, the parent
Out came its child a Plover, and flew
. . .
    REFRAIN
This is the flying place of the bird Halulu
Of Kiwaʻa, the bird that cries over the canoe house
Birds that fly in a flock shutting out the sun
The earth is covered with the fledglings of the night
    breaking into dawn
The time when the dawning light spreads abroad
The young weak ʻape plant rises
A tender plant with spreading leaves
A branching out of the nightborn

Nothing but darkness that
Nothing but darkness this
Darkness alone for Po'ele'ele
A time of dawn indeed for Pohaha
    Still it is night

      The Night-digger

The time arrives for Po-kanokano
To increase the progeny of Po-lalo-uli
Dark is the skin of the new generation
Black is the skin of the beloved Po-lalo-uli
Who sleeps as a wife to the Night-digger
The beaked nose that digs the earth is erected
Let it dig at the land, increase it, heap it up
Walling it up at the back
Walling it up in front
The pig child is born
Lodges inland in the bush
Cultivates the water taro patches of Lo'iloa
Tenfold is the increase of the island
Tenfold the increase of the land
The land where the Night-digger dwelt
Long is the line of his ancestry
The ancient line of the pig of chief blood
The pig of highest rank born in the time
The time when the Night-digger lived
And slept with Po-lalo-uli
    The night gave birth
Born were the peaked-heads, they were clumsy ones
Born were the flat-heads, they were braggarts
Born were the angular-heads, they were esteemed
Born were the fair-haired, they were strangers
Born were the blonds, their skin was white

Born were those with retreating foreheads, they were
    bushy-haired
Born were the blunt-heads, their heads were round
Born were the dark-heads, they were dark
Born were the common class, they were unsettled
Born were the working class, they were workers
Born were the favorites, they were courted
Born were the slave class, and wild was their nature
Born were the cropped-haired, they were the picked
    men
Born were the song chanters, they were indolent
Born were the big bellies, big eaters were they
Born were the timid ones, bashful were they
Born were the messengers, they were sent here and
    there
Born were the slothful, they were lazy
Born were the stingy, they were sour
Born were the puny, they were feeble ones
Born were the thickset, they were stalwart
Born were the broad-chested, broad was their badge
    in battle
Born were the family men, they were home lovers
Born were the mixed breeds, they had no fixed line
    of descent
Born were the lousy-headed, they were lice infested
Born were the war leaders, men followed after them
Born were the high chiefs, they were ruddy
Born were the stragglers, they were dispersed
Scattered here and there
The children of Loʻiloa multiplied
The virgin land sprang into bloom
The gourd of desire was loosened
With desire to extend the family line

To carry on the fruit of Oma's descendants,
The generations from the Night-digger
In that period of the past
    Still it is night

    The nibblers

Many new lines of chiefs spring up
Cultivation arises, full of taboos
They go about scratching at the wet lands
It sprouts, the first blades appear, the food is ready
Food grown by the water courses
Food grown by the sea
Plentiful and heaped up
The parent rats dwell in holes
The little rats huddle together
Those who mark the seasons
Little tolls from the land
Little tolls from the water courses
Trace of the nibblings of these brown-coated ones
With whiskers upstanding
They hide here and there
A rat in the upland, a rat by the sea
A rat running beside the wave
Born to the two, child of the Night-falling-away
Born of the two, child of the Night-creeping-away
The little child creeps as it moves
The little child moves with a spring
Pilfering at the rind
Rind of the 'ohi'a fruit, not a fruit of the upland
A tiny child born as the darkness falls away
A springing child born as the darkness creeps away
Child of the dark and child in the night now here
    Still it is night

The water of Kane

Kane is the major god of the Hawaiian pantheon. The other great gods are Ku, Lono and Kanaloa. The waters of Kane have a special mythical significance. They are the waters of life and are connected with the Hawaiian conception of an earthly paradise, sometimes a floating island, sometimes a place under the sea, sometimes a hidden land where the springs flow and the earth is fruitful.

A query, a question,
I put to you:
Where is the water of Kane?
At the eastern gate
Where the sun comes in at Haehae;
There is the water of Kane.

A question I ask of you:
Where is the water of Kane?
Out with the floating sun,
Where cloud-forms rest on the ocean,
Lifting their forms at Nihoa,
This side of the base of Lehua;
There is the water of Kane.

A question I put to you:
Where is the water of Kane?
There on the mountain peak,
On the steep ridges,
In the valleys,
Where the rivers flow;
There is the water of Kane.

This question I ask of you:
Where, pray, is the water of Kane?
There at sea, on the ocean,
In the driving rain,
In the heavenly rainbow,
In the rising mists,
In the blood-red rainfall,
In the ghostly cloud-form;
There is the water of Kane.

One question I put to you:
Where, where is the water of Kane?
Up on high is the water of Kane,
In the heavenly blue,
In the black-piled cloud,
In the black black cloud,
In the purple blue cloud of the gods;
There is the water of Kane.

One question I ask of you:
Where flows the water of Kane?
Deep in the ground, in the rushing spring,
In the ducts of Kane and Loa,
A wellspring of water to drink,
A water of magic power—
The water of life!
Life! O give us this life!

An appeal for rain

An offering is set apart for you
O Ku of the long cloud, O Ku of the short cloud,
O Ku of the intensely dark clouds of heaven;
From that great black cloud hanging over the
    horizon,
Make fall a heavy shower,
A rain of many small drops,
A rain that moves in columns;
Bring the cultivating rains,
Drench the earth from that boundary to this,
From that side to this,
To soak the soil,
To make our garden fruitful,
To make our plants grow,
So that you may eat of my food with me and my
    family,
So that you may eat of my bananas with me and my
    family,
And be clothed in tapa with me and my family.
'Amama, the kapu of the prayer is freed.

Prayer to Kane

O Kane of the water of life,
Preserve us, thy offspring.

Here is an offering, a hog,
A white fowl, coconuts,
Potatoes, a mana taro.
The power is thine, O Kane,
To collect for us the fish
And relieve the gauntness of the land.
Come in and eat of the feast.
Here is the snout of the pig,
The tail of the pig,
The spleen of the pig,
The neck of the fowl,
The juice of the coconut,
The red sea moss,
The white-leafed mana taro.
'Amama. The kapu of the prayer is freed.

Harvest prayer

O Kane, transform the earth!
Let the earth move as one piece.
The land is cracked and fissured.

The edible fern yet grows, O Lono.
Let kupukupu cover the dry land.
Gather potatoes as stones on the side hills.
The rain comes like the side of a cliff,
The rain falling from heaven.
The potato also falls from heaven,
The wild taro is the only taro now,
The taro of the mountain patches.
The only food is that of the wilds,
    O Kane!

O Kane and Lono! Gods of the husbandmen,
Give life to the land!
Until the food goes to waste,
Until it sprouts in the ground,
Until the leaves cover the land;
Such be the plenty
Of you, O Kane and Lono.
'Amama. The kapu of the prayer is freed.

House dedication prayer

Cut the umbilical cord of the house
A house that resists rain and storm.
A house for man to dwell in.
O Lono, behold the house,
A house in the presence of the giver of life,
Grant life to those who live there,
Grant life to visitors that come,
Grant life to the landlord,
Grant life to the chiefs,
Let it be life from the life-giver,
Life until one creeps and is weak-eyed with age
Until one sprawls like a withered hala leaf
Until one reaches the end of life.
Let this be the life granted to us by the gods.

O Ku, O Kane, O Lono,
Let down the gift of life,
And all the blessings with it.
Till heaven and earth are heaped,
Let them be raised up by Kane of the living waters.
May there be life from one boundary to the other
From above to below
From roof to foundation.
May there be life—everlasting life.

Tree-felling song

They bear the god's ax up the mountain;
Trampling the mud, like waves from Kahiki
That beat on the rim of Kilauea.
The people with offerings lift up a prayer;
A woman strings wreaths in Olaa—
My lehua grove bordering He-eia.
And now Kukuena, mother god,
Dresses in a ti-leaf skirt;
She mounts the altar; she sits.
Here we are, your many priests.
Enter in, possess us!

Pele and Hi'i-aka

The Pele and Hi'i-aka cycle of chants and legends takes on epic qualities in its length and its revelation of the Hawaiian voice. The poems show the Hawaiian concern for the primal elements of sea, fire, land: they reveal also a tie with landscape which is at once human and mythic. The story tells of Pele's settling in Kīlauea on the island of Hawai'i. During a deep sleep her spirit leaves her and goes to Kaua'i where she falls in love with a young chief, Lohi'au. Upon awakening, Pele sends her sister Hi'i-aka to bring Lohi'au to her. Hi'i-aka asks Pele to take care of her lehua forests while she is away. Hi'i-aka makes a voyage filled with encounters and dangers, a classic voyage out and voyage of return. Many of the poems of the cycle are a telling of the adventures of the journey. When she reaches the island of Kaua'i, she finds that Lohi'au is dead. She restores his life and begins the return. Pele betrays Hi'i-aka and destroys her red-blossomed forests. Hi'i-aka, distraught, makes love to Lohi'au on the edge of the crater Kīlauea. The fire goddess kills Lohi'au. But again he is restored to life.

The coming of Pele

The color red is associated with Pele as goddess of the volcano.

From Kahiki came the woman Pele,
from the land of Polapola,
from the rising reddish mist of Kāne,
from clouds blazing in the sky, horizon clouds.
Restless desire for Hawai'i seized the woman Pele.
Ready-carved was the canoe, Honua-i-Ākea,
your own canoe, O Ka-moho-ali'i,
for sailing to distant lands.

Well-lashed and equipped, the canoe of high gods,
your canoe, Sacred-hewer-of-the-land,
stood ready to sail with the ocean current.

Pele-honua-mea embarked, the heavenly one
stepped aboard to sail round Kahiki island.
Multitudes of gods came aboard.

O royal companions, who handled the steering
    paddle at the stern?
Pele-the-redhead herself was helmswoman, ruler of
    the Menehune.
Ku and Lono bailed out the bilge water,
carried paddles, placed them in station.

Hiʻi-aka, the wise sister, next embarked,
boarded the craft to dwell with Pele in her sailing
    quarters,
close to Pele on the long voyage.

Jets of lava gushed from Kahiki.
Pele hurled her lightning,
vomit of flame, outpouring of lava was the woman's
    farewell.

The spy

Early in her journey to bring Lohi'au to Pele, Hi'i-aka travels through a dangerous forest, the domain of a lizard goddess. She recognizes that a watching bird is a spy who tempts her to drink awa, a liquor.

The bird that sips lehua honey,
Yellow awa collected
In the uplands of Ka-li'u;
The bird that carries the leaf of awa,
The bitter plant of Puna:
Her love pours sweetly forth
urging me continuously to sleep.
O tide of sleep!

Watch your way

Though the awa cup is a temptation, Hiʻi-aka realizes she must not sleep. She expresses this in song.

Watch your way in upland Puna.
Don't pick a single flower—
You might stray from the path.
A shape is hidden beneath a stone.
Flowers cover the path,
It moves on overgrown stones—
Swift the downfall!
Is there love between us?
Go! Enter the house of Pele!
Erupt, Kahiki; flash, lightning!
Pele, burst forth!

Songs of the girl without hands

On Maui Hi'i-aka meets a girl without hands who is gathering shellfish. She dances with the waves and sings. She is, in reality, a spirit.

I love the fish of my land
Caught by the light of the torch,
The handsome fish embraced by women.
Lost is my companion,
The night is cold:
O love which came for just a day!
O Kona, my land of calm!

A wave knocks the basket of fish from her arms and she sings of her loss.

My fish dance on the waves,
My arm danced from the basket:
An artful dancer sways at noon,
Muting the roar of the sea.
Gone are my fish,
Snatched from my arms.
Gone, gone!

She sees a shark.

O little fish with wicked eye,
With blunt nose, that swims the ocean,
Fish that darts and strikes,
That lashes in the dark blue sea.
Alas, the great shark has destroyed me!

Stormy weather

Hiʻi-aka has reached the island of Oʻahu. She sings of the stormy weather of Koʻolau.

Blustery is the weather of Koʻolau!
One soaks and swells in Koʻolau rain,
It pours at Ma-eli-eli,
It gutters the land at He-eia;
It lashes the sea with a whip.
The rain dances in joy
At ʻĀhui-manu; shifting,
It shakes the heaps of coral.
The rain circles round and round at Kaha-luʻu.
I am troubled and sad,
My eyes are full of tears.
Tears overflow.

Kauhi

Hiʻi-aka comes to a deep narrow gorge. She sees the shape of an ancestor, Kauhi, in the rock forms. The eyes are shining with dew and seem to look at her with longing. Manuʻu-ke-eu is a mythical pandanus tree.

Kauhi, watchtower of the sky,
Cliff, twisted and fluted,
O mountain precipice,
Slippery to climb as Ka-liʻu-waʻa,
Or the ranging heights of Puna and Hilo.
O the hala fruits of Manuʻu-ke-eu,
Let me string a lei to wear:
Kauhi, hung with flowers and ferns;
The eye of the god,
The eye of the bat, Peʻapeʻa.
As a bird, ruffle your plumage,
Fly, soar as a kite;
Taking the wind, taking the rain,
Your feathers like the seagull's,
Sail on the wings of a god.
He is a god, yet he does not hear;
A great wrath in his eyes.
He wakes, he wakes.
He wakes and turns to me.
Awake, you who face the heavens,
Awake, you who bring winter rain,
Awake!

Hi'i-aka's song at Ka-'ena

Ka-'ena reaches out like a bird flying overhead,
a sea gannet soaring in a still sky
above sandy Nēnē-le'a,
a bo'sunbird high over the channel of Ka-'ie'ie—
a flapping of wings.

Like a thirsty man drinking from a pool
so do rocks near Ka-'ena drink of foamy waves.
Silent pounding has darkened those quiet faces of
    stone.
Bruised black and red, waterworn,
they have grown ghostly from long attending the sea
    of Kāpeku,
a wintry season's song.

Blackened and red from perpetual pounding
stand these sea-wardens of the land:
naked god-forms, unstable god-forms,
assumed by Kanaloa who shaped them,
sea-washed bird-forms of the high god
guarding the shore at Cape Ka-lā'au,
sprayed by the sea of Ewelua.

In cliff-steep gullies at Unulau
I too drink of Kā-'apu's water.
(The countryman, with surly denial, would hide it
    from strangers.)
Yet at Ka-'ena four shy streamlets wind seaward
in heat of summer sun.

Their living waters file before me in parade.
Lei-honua's great wall beholds the procession.

With the rising of the wind I am caught by a sudden
    thought.
What shall I, in my shame, give to the four bathers?

My sole gift is a song.

Hi'i-aka's song for the Stone of Kaua'i

Ka-'ena's brine-parched shore bakes in the sun.
Streaked with flame, consumed, the great rock
    transformed
sails into stillness, the sea's calm.

Sand holes sink underfoot. Coral heads twist upward
quickened into life by the traveler wind Mālua,
sea-borne companion of mine from Ko'olau.
When Ko'olau blows inland shaggy plains bristle.

"Speed!" shouts the sailor to his canoe.
"Speed on, while Nēnē-le'a's sands lie still.
Here's no beating against storm blast,
only Mālua's light sea-slap along the bow."

O foolish sailor boy, forgetting how hungry waves
    devour
staunchest rocks!

Stone of Kaua'i, you've manned this watch for ages.
Hold firm, kinsman mine.
Endure, old settler.

Songs to the ghost of Lohiʻau

Hiʻi-aka reaches Kauaʻi. She sees a ghostly figure standing before a cave. She chants two songs to the ghost of Lohiʻau.

This surely is not the man,
Not the lover for the evening,
Not the companion to love
In the long darkness of a winter's night.
My man, where? Where are you?

My man of the light and windy rain,
Of the cold rain of the mountain,
The mountain steeps at Ka-lalau
Where we go together.
With you, my friend, my love,
My companion of the darkness
When my face looks up—
My man, oh my man!

Hi'i-aka chants to restore Lohi'au to life

Hi'i-aka performs rituals for Lohi'au. This is one of the mele-pule which she chants. Uli is the goddess of sorcery and healing.

Speed, O Uli, this prayer for health;
Speed it to the brightness of heaven.
Ask the demigods above;
Who are the demigods above?
The blue cloud of the sky,
The white cloud, the red cloud;
The god Ku of the small cloud
Ku of the long cloud
Ku of the mackerel cloud
Ku of the red and ragged cloud in the sky.
The small gods of the mountains,
Our companions of the shady forest;
The goddesses of healing,
The god Laka who gives ripe mountain-apples.
The gods pour their healing water;
The pili grass waves;
The echo sounds in the distance.
. . .
I, Hi'i-aka, come
From love of my sister—
Be this a place of birth!
O life, give life!

Vision of the burning

Hiʻi-aka starts the return journey to Kīlauea with Lohiʻau. On the island of Oʻahu she climbs the slopes of Diamond Head and sees, with her special power, the burning of her ohia trees on the island of Hawaiʻi. Pele has broken her pledge.

Fire-split rocks strike the sun;
Fire pours on the sea at Puna;
The bright sea at Kū-kiʻi.
The gods of the night at the eastern gate,
The skeleton woods that loom.
What is the meaning of this?
The meaning is desolation.

A storm, a rough surf

Hiʻi-aka takes revenge for the broken pledge. On the edge of the crater of Kīlauea she approaches Lohiʻau with love. The wrathful Pele pours fire on Lohiʻau. Hiʻi-aka bids him pray. The Puʻu-lena wind suggests sulphur.

A storm, a rough surf in Kīlauea Pit,
Combers of fire threatening, breaking;
Flame splashes the lehua buds—
The sound of Hiku, the woman who consumes lehua,
Who destroys the altar of fishermen,
The stone, clawed by fire, breaks;
The Puʻu-lena wind strikes;
The island shakes and trembles;
A flood of rain in the lowland,
A cold wind in the upland.
A thunder boom from this cliff,
A distant hum from that cliff,
A soft breath from Kua-loi mountain—
The home of the gods,
The shrine of the god Ka-hoa-lii.
The voice of the ohia rises,
The voice of the sea cries,
The plates of fire turn upward.
The sea shakes hala trees at Keaʻau
The sea scatters lehua bloom at Pana-ʻewa
It breaks over the altar of Lono.
Does she hear me? She is deaf,
Deaf to my sighs, she does not listen.

The fires of Pele

In his suffering Lohiʻau hallucinates. Wai-wela-wela is a hot lake in Puna.

The stars, the moon are on fire;
The cold months burn;
Dust circles on the island, the land is parched.
The sky hangs low, rough seas in the pit—
The ocean tosses; lava surges in Kīlauea.
Waves of fire cover the plain;
Pele erupts.
A crash of thunder brings rain from the sky;
The earth quakes; the thunder roars.
Once Puna was majestic;
Now clouds of omen hang low.
Foam looms over the fire of Laka.
Wai-wela-wela is a warm skirt.
I choke in lehua smoke—
The heavy stench of burnt man!
I am without breath, covered with fire;
O Hiʻi-aka, cry your tears!

Lohiʻau's song

Lohiʻau is restored to life by a brother of Pele who, on his voyage from Kahiki (Tahiti), saw Lohiʻau's spirit fluttering over the water. He captured the spirit.

I lived, but I was a spirit without body.
Then came the king of Kahiki,
The king who sails the dark blue sea,
The black sea, the yellow sea,
The purple, the red brown sea of Kane.
The flooding sea of the Chief Hinaliʻi—
The silent sea, the floating sea.
Lohiʻau flowers in the daylight.
It is I, Lohiʻau; do you hear?
O life, new life for Lohiʻau,
Yes, for Lohiʻau.

From "Fallen is the chief"

By Keaulumoku. This poem, in fifteen cantos, is famous as a prophecy of the overthrow of Keoua by King Kamehameha the Great. The chief named in the first line is Kamehameha. "They" refers to the people of the districts he has conquered.

from Canto III

The chief takes hold, the work is done.
He bends his back—they are thrown into darkness;
They push each other on every side; with broken
    bones they chase each other;
The bones of the island are broken, the bones of the
    land creak;
Broken, they creak like a falling cliff.
The enemy gasps, he doubles up in pain, the air
    around him is hot;
They move uncertainly. Sideways in the air they fall
    like a kite.
The kingdom has become the toenail of the island;
Chin above, top of the head below,
Swinging back and forth.
Hawaii is a swing; it is like the rope that pulls the
    swing;
They are routed by the followers of the chief, by this
    chief.
They looked this way and that, afraid in the forest
While the slaughter raged; no one is spared.
They moved swiftly as a stream through a narrow
    opening—

Like the burning oven of Pele
When the steam rises to the sky;
Like the constant restlessness of the high surf
When the soft and hard coral are thrown on the
    beach,
So thrown together, the refuse of the island.

   from Canto IV

To the chief belongs the island, the land,
The chief holds the uplands and the ocean;
For him is the night, for him the day,
For him are the winter and the summer,
The month, the seven stars of heaven now in view.
All precious property, above and below,
The chief holds all fixed property;
All property that floats ashore, all birds that light
    upon the land,
The thick-shelled broad-backed turtle, the whale ivory
And the yearly uhu fish.
Chief of the highest rank! Let him live forever!
Let him be borne with honor among the short gods
    and the long gods.
Let him go forth in peace, the chief who possesses the
    island.
Prepare the dance on the dance ground;
Let the dancers rise and fall throughout the islands.

From "A chant for the island of Maui"

By Keaulumoku

Let the rain fall, for rain is good.
It patters down, it pelts down,
It crushes the forest growth,
It sprinkles musically on the lehua.
The lehua trees blossom, the yellow lehua,
When the rain comes to Kailua.
The petals are heavy with raindrops,
Heavy and full-blown.
They do not know the thirst
That wilts the first-blown pandanus bloom.
Rain returns by way of Hane-hoʻi,
Along the brow of Puʻumaile to Hoalua,
Over the ridge of Puʻukoaʻe,
Before the face of the cliff of Huelo.
There it pours down on Kaumealani,
The rain that brings out the full-blown flowers
And draws them close down to the shore.
The rain goes out to sea,
It falls on Hawini like teardrops,
It passes along over the headlands,
It creeps by the cliffs and capes
Creeps by the cape of Mokupapa.
. . .

Oh for the light summer showers
That brought forth the blossoms!
The blossoms droop with stems half-broken,
The blossoms hang wilted, uncared for;
The fruit clusters, ripened above,
Mildew and fall in piles to the ground;
both fruit and flowers are mildewed.
Hala fruit and mountain apples drop in the stream
And are washed down in the water of Kakipi,
Washed up on thorny weeds,
On the flowers of coarse grasses
Where we two have wandered,
My wife and I, to the rain-wet hala grove of Kuloli,
Fragrant among the leaves,
The hala leaves over the resting place of Koʻolahale,
Where we watched for the belated moon
To rise over the cinder cone of Malama.

A kapu is placed

From the legend of Halemano. Halemano chants two songs to his estranged wife.

I

The fire of Laka places a kapu over the roads of Puna;
I see its reflection in my eyes.
It is like the breadfruit in the lowlands of Kookoolau;
I am almost tempted to pick it.
Filled with shame, I do not touch it.
Alas, my love!
My love from the broad sea of Puna
Whose waves beat on the sea cliffs,
You forgot your lover when you went astray in
    Kaimu,
Your mouth was silent, you did not call.
My love of the house where we were friendless,
The house to which we had no right, though I did
    not complain,
Where I was warmed by the sun at Maliu,
Listen as I call—
My own, my love!

2

The sea is cutting down the hala trees of Puna,
They stand like men,
Like a crowd in the lowlands of Hilo.
The sea surges, flooding Mokuola.
I am alive again for love of you,
For anger is a helper to man.
As I walked, friendless, along the roads
That way and this way, what of me my love?
Alas, my own dear love!
My companion of the low-hanging breadfruit of
    Kalapana,
Of the cold sun that rises at Kumukahi.
The love of a wife is above all else,
For my head is burning,
My navel is tingling with love,
My body is in bond to her.
Come back to me, my companion of Koolau,
My love, come back.

Love song

Though on the surface this poem paints a landscape, its inner meaning concerns a love affair filled with anger and abuse.

Lehua flower that reddens the sea of Kona,
The sea dyed red with scarlet,
The red-glowing sea;
The uplands of Alaea are red;
The kapa of the women is dyed the red of fire,
Stirred by gossip, tossed by love.
The bright waterway shines with dew,
The dew which lies on the coconut fronds.
The foliage of the trees, the long leaves—
They wilt in the heat of Kailua, the deep.
A narrow and dusty mat spread out,
A slope of land by the calm sea.
Mount Kilohana looms—
Your wooded slopes, your name continues,
Your tabu is gone! Your forbidden ridge has been
    climbed,
It has been stepped upon, conquered.

The salt pond of Mana

This is part of a name song for the chiefess Ohaikawiliula. Mana on the island of Kauai is celebrated for the beautiful mirages of its salt pond.

The salt pond of Mana
Is breaking away.
The water is breaking away—
The water of Kamakahou is breaking away.
Salt is the water,
The water of Mana.
Like the sea is the water,
Like water is the sea,
Like the sea is the water of Kamakahou.
The land which I enjoyed and rejected and forsook—
It has gone before,
It is forgotten,
It has gone, both back and front.
The iliau bush has faded in the sunlight,
As the heavy dew of the morning.
The emblems of the god of the year have passed,
Gone to bury the dead,
On the barren sands of Nonohili.
. . .

From "Ka-'ahu-manu's dirge for Ke'e-au-moku"

The blazing fire in the last stanza alludes to the bedmate.

My father and chief,
My beloved companion,
My loved one.
I am breathless with grieving for you,
I weep for my companion in the cold,
My companion of the chilly rain.

The chill encircles me,
The cold surrounds me,
Purple with cold not rejected,

Only two places to find warmth—
The blazing fire within the house,
The tapa covering is the second warmth,
Found in the bosom of a companion.
It is there, it is there, it is there.

From "Birth chant for Kau-i-ke-ao-uli"

Kau-i-ke-ao-uli was Kamehameha III. His birth is connected with the origin of things. Kea, or Wākea, and Papa are the first man and woman, progenitors of the chiefs. Wākea is the sky-father and Papa the earth-mother.

I

The chiefess gave birth,
she bore in labor above,
she lay as in a faint, a weakness at the navel.
The afterbirth stirred at the roots, crept in darkness,
in waves of pain came the bitter bile of the child.
This was a month of travail,
of gasping labor,
a writhing to deliver the chief.
He is this chief, born of a chiefess.

Now a chief shall be here above.
Who shall be below?

Born was the earth, rooted the earth.
The root crept forth, rootlets of the earth.
Royal rootlets spread their way through the earth to
    hold firm.
Down too went the taproot, creaking
like the mainpost of a house, and the earth moved.
Cliffs rose upon the earth, the earth lay widespread:

a standing earth, a sitting earth was the earth,
a swaying earth, a solid earth was the earth.
The earth lay below, from below the earth rose.
The earth was Kea's, to Kea belonged the earth.
The earth was Papa's, to Papa belonged the earth,
the earthly firstborn borne by Papa.
He is this earth, the earth that was born.

The earth shall be here below.
Who shall be above?

2

Born was the night above,
born was the night up here.
The heavens slid away into the night, swift came the
    afterbirth.
The nights came closer together, stretching along
until a separation came, making distinct the night of
    Mahina-leʻa.
The night turned, closeness became separated.
This is the royal offspring of night borne by Kea,
first child of the night, second child of the night,
third child of the night.
The night lay in travail
to give birth to the night.
He is this night, the night newly born.

Who shall be below?
Who shall be upon the island?

3
Born was the island, it grew, it sprouted,
it flourished, lengthened, rooted deeply, budded,
    formed tender leaves.
That was the island over Hawai'i.
Hawai'i itself was an island.
The land was unstable, Hawai'i quivered,
moved freely about in space,
Wākea recognized the island, Hawai'i recognized
    remained.
Visible were island and earth,
held in heavenly space by the right hand of Wākea,
Hawai'i was held, Hawai'i was seen, an island.

Down here shall be an island.
Who shall be above—Who?
The cloud, that is who it shall be. . . .

A name song for Princess Nahiʻenaʻena

A name chant for the princess,
For Nahiʻenaʻena a name!
Chief among women!
She warms the cold wind with her flame;
A peace that is mirrored in calm;
A wind that sheds rain;
A tide that flowed long ago;
The water spring of Mana,
Life-spring for the people,
Where the snarling dog
Bites and barks at the sea.
The spray drifts on the bloom
Of the ili-au flower
The scarlet flower of ohai,
On the mat of wild grass,
Woven with fern and long rushes.
The spouting-horn, Kawelo-hea,
Asks, "Who of right has the tabu?
The princess Nahiʻenaʻena!"
The flowers glow in the pool,
The bathing pool of Holei!

Song

This poem can be a description of a hard climb up a mountain, or it can be a landscape which suggests a passionate love affair.

The climb to Hanalei woods is steep—
To tread on clumps of grass over the swamp;
To cling to the ledges
And cling to the ladder of hanging roots.
The buttocks of my companion swing over me,
His loins are exhausted;
Two beautiful forms!
Sheltered from rain, I crouch under this bank.

Shark song

In this poem the shark is the god of love.

Alas, I am seized by the great shark!
The white fins and triple-banked teeth.
The foundation of Lono is gone—
Torn up by the monster shark
Niuhi with eyes of fire
That flash in the blue black sea.
Auwe! Auwe!
When the wili-wili tree blooms
Then the shark god bites.
Auwe! I am seized by the great shark!
O blue sea, O black sea,
The purple blue sea of Kane!
The joy of my dancing!
Alas! consumed by the great shark!

Chant composed while drunk

By John Papa Ii

The clouds appear yellow over the sea,
A sea that is the color of the clear sky.
The 'ulae fishers sail out in the calm,
The keel can be seen.
A sky is reflected from above,
Shadows are cast by the forest,
Covering the brow of the mountain;
They move before my eyes,
The light appears in patches like 'oloa tapa.
Night descends and I am drowsy,
I am overcome by sleep.
A damp coldness rouses me,
I am chilled with the cold of Kawanui,
With the dew that fills the canoe hulls of Maihi
In the distant upland of Hainoa.

Lament on the death of a first child

By Pa'ahana

This is a dirge, an expression of affection,
For you, O Miss Mary Binning,
My daughter in the dust-scattering wind of Na'alehu,
In the home we shared together,
Oh—my daughter!
My daughter at the cliff of Lau-hu;
Love for you makes my tears flow unchecked,
Oh my daughter at the cold spring of Ka-puna,
A beloved place to which we went,
My daughter in the rain that passes the hill of Ha'ao,
A place we were fond of going together,
We used to go up the long trail,
A little known trail, unattended by a friend.
Oh my darling—how sad I am at losing you.
You have gone on a road on which there is no
    returning,
Oh my darling—my pet.
My constant companion in the homeland,
Here I remain
With this great load, a yearning for you,
Oh my darling, precious as a necklace of pearls,
My daughter in the warm sun of Waikapuna,
Beloved is that place where we used to go.
My daughter among the fragrant flowers,
Oh my necklace, my golden chain, farewell—alas!

From "A name chant for Kupake'e"

I do not care for Kona,
For Ka-'u is mine.
The water from Kalae is carried all night long,
Wrung from tapas and sponges.
This land is heard of as having no water,
Except the water waited for at Mana and Unulau.
Much prized water is found in the eye socket of the
    fish,
The water prized and cared for by the man.
The child carries a gourd container in his arms.
It whistles, whistles as the wind blows into it,
the voice of the water gourd is produced by the wind
Sounding like a nose flute at midnight.
The long-drawn whistling of the gourd, we hear.
Listen, how fortunate you are!
There is no going back, our ways are different.
In childhood only does one regret in secret,
Grieving alone.
Look forward with love to the season ahead of us.
Let the season pass that is gone.

Song of the chanter Ka-'ehu

What will become of Hawai'i?
What will leprosy do to our land—
disease of the despised, dreaded alike
by white or brown or darker-skinned?

Strange when a man's neighbors
become less than acquaintances.
Seeing me they drew away.
They moved to sit elsewhere, whispering,
and a friend pointed a finger:
"He is a leper."

I bowed my head.
I knew it was true.
In my heart I hugged my shame.

Word reached the medical authorities.
The doctors sent the military to fetch us.
We were caught like chickens, like cattle herded
along roadway and country land.
Then they paraded us before the Board of Health
But there was no health in that Board for such as we.
Examining doctors eyed us, squinted this way and
      that.
More fingers pointed Diamond Head way:
"You go to Kala-wao!"

Again the militia took over.
Soldiers escorted us to the wharf for farewell.
Prisoners, we were marched aboard,
victims of leprosy, branded for exile.
Abandoned, cut off from family and dear ones,
we were left alone with our grief, with our love.
Rain of tears streamed from leper eyes.
Leper cheeks glistened with raindrops in the sun.
Never again would we look upon this land of ours,
this lovely harbor town.

Quickly the sails were hoisted.
Ropes dangled from the foremast,
tails of wild animals writhing,
whipping in the channel breeze.
The *John Bull* drew anchor.
In the stern the rudder turned.
So sailed we forth to dim Molokaʻi Island,
enshrouded in fog.

So ends my song and this refrain.
What will leprosy do to my people?
What will become of our land?

Piano at evening

By Palea. He composed the chant immediately after hearing a piano for the first time.

O piano I hear at evening,
where are you?

Your music haunts me far into the night
like the voice of landshells
trilling sweetly
near the break of day.

I remember when my dear and I
visited aboard the *Nautilus*
and saw our first looking glass.

I remember the upland of Ma'eli'eli
where the mists creeping in and out
threaded their way between the old
houses of thatch.

Again I chant my refrain
of long ago and a piano singing
far into the night.

Samoa

From a creation chant

This section of the poem tells of the origin of man from the "peopling vine."

Now the sacred vine starts life,
But its children only wriggle in the sun;
They have no legs, no arms,
No head, no face,
No beat of heart!
The god Tagaloa, descending to the west
Speaks, and it is done:
"These fruits, the product of the vine, are worms,
But I fashion them into forms with limbs;
I now give a will to each;
Your bodies must remain opaque,
Your faces must shine
To entertain Tagaloa
When he comes to walk this earth."

Chant for the whale

Pou sets out on a voyage to Hawaiki to get sweet potatoes. He uses a whale named "Wise Man" for a canoe. As he jumps on the whale's back, he chants.

Dive! Disappear below the surface.
With swelling of the heart
Urged on to the ancient of the heavens,
Arise at the summit,
Arise to the daylight
At the island landfall.
It's once, it's once, it's twice, it's twice
It's thrice, it's thrice,
A fish worn down at the ancient of the heavens.
Arise, arise at the summit,
Arise to the daylight,
Arise at the island landfall
To reach the surface at the landfall Marua-nuku.
With determination the shore is reached,
And a landing made on the sands of Hawaiki.

Lovers' farewell

There are many stories of Sina and her family. In this one a man with the body of an eel is her lover. The two flee from the anger of her family. Finally the eel man is killed. As he is dying, he sings this song. Later a coconut tree springs from his grave.

Sina, let us part in love.
When I am killed,
Ask for my head as your portion.
Take and plant it in a stone wall.
You will drink its fruit
And use it as water carriers, single and double.
With its leaves you will plait mats and roofing,
And make a fan to fan yourself
When meditating on your love for me.
You will see my face in the coconuts
And kiss it each time you drink.

Tonga

The weather shore of Vavau

In recitative style.

    We were talking about the weather shore of Vavau when the women said to us,
    "Let us walk to the weather side to watch the sunset, listen to the singing of the birds and the lamentations of the wood pigeon.
    We will gather flowers near the cliff of Matawto,
    We will stay and share the provisions brought us from Likuone,
    We will bathe in the sea, rinse in the water of the roots and anoint ourselves with sweet-scented oil,
    We will string flowers and plait the ti we pick at Matawto.
    While we stand on the precipice at Bird Cave, we will look breathless on the distant sea below.
    As we are lost in thought, the great wind whistles toward us from the tall casuarinas inland on the plains.
    My thought rises watching the surf below trying to tear away the firm rocks.
    It is evening. Let us go to the village.
    Listen! I hear a band of singers. Are they practicing a hula to dance at the malae at Tanea? Let us go there. It will remind us of other festivals before our land was torn by war.
    War is terrible! Look how weeds take over the land. How sad that many men are dead.

Our chiefs remain disturbed; they do not often wander alone by moonlight to visit their mistresses.

Enough of these thoughts! How can we help being at war? The land of Fiji has brought war to our land of Tonga. Let us act like Fijians.

Enough of sadness! Tomorrow we may be dead.

Let us decorate ourselves with red dye and bind our waists with fine white tapa. We will crown ourselves with wreaths of fragrant gardenias and wear necklaces of huni flowers to show off our sun-reddened skins.

Listen to the praise of the people. Now the hula has ended; they are portioning out the food of the feast.

Let us go tomorrow to the village.

The young men beg eagerly for our flower wreaths. They flatter us: 'How beautiful these girls look coming from the weather shore! How beautiful their sun-reddened skins; their fragrance like the flowers at the precipice, at the lookout.'

I am anxious to go to the weather side. Let us go tomorrow.''

Love song

Blossoms of tetefa and budding of siale,
Ah, my dear queen's longing that she be exalted;
Oh, my heart is pained by our separation,
Death's own self would not be to me such sore
    agony.
A-e.

Am I a siale that my bloom should open?
Or am I a tropic bird that I soar afar?
Oh, my heart is pained by our separation,
Death's own self would not be to me such sore
    agony.
A-e.

How I love her way

By Tangatailoa

How I love her way,
Love her way that is hers alone,
Little green pigeon still unlearned;
The pigeon we're seeking is a maiden.
Tug at the cord to entrap her.
My joy is the pigeon who flees as the shadow.
He a e he.
Bead or ivory or floating star,
Girdle or scented wreath.
A venturesome bird is woman,
I turned away and was grieved;
Not for ever is her careless chatter,
No matter what strange thing may happen.
The eastern shore is weary of wonder
About its man, where he may be.
Tell them my joy is in dance and love,
The road of the siale has kept me;
On my neck the string of sweet blossoms,
My belt entwined with siale.
If Inumomea asks about me,
Tell him Mulikihaamea
Is still the most handsome of men,
And his kindliness has been moved
To be forgetful of Vaea.
Tell the king that they seek me,
Set the course by the village Lakepa,

The stars, Maukuomaa and Tapukitea,
Alotolu and Kaukupenga,
Tapuatamata and the flowers, hingaroleka,
Unuoisiale and tetefa,
And bring Aoouvea
To adorn her for a night of dancing.
How I love her way.

Poem of Falepapalangi to Mamaeaepoto

Falepapalangi and Mamaeaepoto were famous poets of the first half of the nineteenth century. They often composed in rivalry with each other. When the poet speaks of the gull seeking its food, he is saying metaphorically that the poet searches for subjects.

Ah, surely a most laughable thing
Is sitting around Tonga and the isles
While you ask one another of me:
Have I been concerned in declaring a war?
Or broken the sacredness of a gift?
Or been defeated at the Sacred Reef?
You may say moreover you're a poet,
But you are foolish in his art,
And you do not remember.
There is no other but I
Who am skilled on the left hand and the right
When Tongatabu makes ready the dance.
Leave a poor little poem of mine
For Haapai and Vavau to take,
And leave it in Houmahaaloau,
Take it around to Anamanu;
For you have shaken your hand—
You have given up—
In the place Falalatokelau.
I came to shore freshly bathed *e*,
And cut toa and feifai *e*,

And there came my summons to the court at
    Pangai *e*
That they might see this skill of mine *e*,
For I had come from Vaoai *e*,
And the king's majesty spoke to me *e*,
That I should not gird myself with a mat *e*,
But deck myself with the fatai *e*,
And tell my poem at his bathing place *e*,
Before their face in Onevai *e*.
Ah me, ah me, the censure.
Be at ease in your justification,
For I take no thought of blame;
I heard from the windward canoe,
It is said in the song of the deck,
And I communed with my heart—
There's a chief being whispered about.
Has the mound of Kafoa been deserted?
Teach a poem about it.
Do you blame kava that I should be drunk?
An ocean that I should swim?
Am I a rainbow that I should not be?
A tern who is wearied in flight?
A siale to burst into bloom?
Should I eat turned away in respect?
Am I not even as you?
Between us the relation of men?
Like the quarrel of husband and wife,
They part but cannot forget.
The decision is with the chief,
Who will then let him know.
A bird, the gull, sought its food,
Came to shore and slept on a headland:

For I am a beach where all meet.
Take the poem *e*,
Put it aboard a canoe *e*,
To take it to Akana *e*,
Or to Tamatuitala *e*,
Anyone who likes it *e*,
Then let him keep it for himself *e*,
That he may speak in friendship with it *e*,
In the Place-of-mutual-liking *e*,
Where the huni blooms,
The hau gleams,
In Vavau on the line of headlands.

Poem of Veehala

Veehala, a poet, is disturbed by the gossip circulating about him. There is, perhaps, a charge against him which could bring death. The meaning is not clear. Matamoana and the Sacred Reef are metaphors for the chief who protects. The man who goes early to fish for bonito is a metaphor for the wise man who approaches the chief with a presentation. When the poet speaks of wishing to be a war vessel which has not heard of the book left in Hihifo (the Bible) he is talking of a man who wishes he were a person of the old days.

It's a thing that has no end,
The talk and questioning about me.
Fear has risen in me,
And, despairing, I remember
This body of mine, so sweet,
Which is joined with a mention of death.
Were there a crime to be discovered,
Or a thing I had taken
Which is continually being sought—
But how should one forget
Matamoana, still haunted by pigeons,
And the Sacred Reef, where still there are fish?
Whoever has wise understanding
Goes early at the waning moon;
The rod is set on the handle
Because of the rising bonito;
The oar vainly strikes the waves
Trying to row swiftly.
Alas!
I am amazed
At this much talked about nothing.

If it were put in a boat she would sink,
If it were on a tree it would fall.
I wish I were a war vessel
Cruising the distant sea,
Not hearing the report
Of the book left in Hihifo
By the generation that was wise.
It was done in the way of the foolish,
And, look, it has come to the assembly.

The Society Islands

Creation chant

He abides—Taaroa is his name—
In the immensity of space.
There was no earth, no heaven,
There was no sea, no mankind.
Taaroa calls on high;
He changes completely.
Taaroa is the root,
The rock—the foundation—
Taaroa is the sand;
He stretches out branches.
Taaroa is the light,
He is within,
He is below;
Taaroa is enduring,
He is wise.
He created the land of Hawaii—
Hawaii the great and sacred,
A shell for Taaroa.
The earth is dancing.
O foundation, O rock
O sands, here.
Brought here, press together the earth.
Press, press again!
Stretch out the seven heavens; let ignorance cease.
Create the heavens, let darkness cease.
Let anxiety cease within;
Let repose cease;
Let the period of messengers cease;
It is the time of the speaker.

Fill up the foundations,
Fill up the rocks,
Fill up the sands.
The heavens are surrounding,
And hung up are the heavens
In the depths;
Finished be the world of Hawaii.

Chant for a royal birth

Lay hold of the cord of the child,
The sacred cord
Of the god that has flown hither.
Let it be long a cord of life;
Tie it firmly with thread;
Then sever the cord of the child god
With the sacred knife of the flying bamboo,
Perforate the cord, the vigorous cord
That the godly cord be light.

Anointing the royal child

This is the purifier, the heart of the banana,
Banana tree of the gods,
To pass over the smooth skin,
The tender skin of the child.
Anoint with oil of sweet odor
The body of this child god
That it be soft, that it be glossy
With the sacred oil of the gods.
Squeeze dry, and saturate with oil
The cord that is flexible, be dry,
For a garland for the neck of the child
Encircle the neck with the cord
As a garland a pledge of long life,
For the child god here present.

Chant to usher in the dawn

The clouds are bordering the sky,
The clouds are awake!
There are rising clouds
That climb in the morning,
Clouds that are carried—
Floating are those dark clouds,
Perfectly formed
And lifted from 'Oro-pa'a,
Lord of the ocean.
In the shades of night
The clouds that rise pile up,
The clouds condense,
Form an archway for the sun.
The clouds are wafted—
They are perfected early
And lifted from 'Oro-pa'a,
The lord of the ocean.
In the shades of night
The clouds rise, and part,
Condense, and reunite
Into an arch of red clouds,
For the sun as it rises
From 'Oro-pa'a of the ocean.

The song of Ru's sister

Ru, who raised the sky from the earth, and his sister Hina set out in a canoe to explore the earth. Hina in the bow of the canoe sings.

O depths of the rivers!
O coldness of the rivers!
Little shrimp of the rivers,
Great shrimp of the rivers,
O prawns of the rivers,
O fullness of the rivers!
The waters inland reflecting flowers
That approach and withdraw!
Let the farsighted who dwell on land
Arise and see!
Look inland to the settled mountains!
Let the farsighted who dwell on land
Arise and see!
Look over the sea of Te-fatu-moana!
Let the farsighted who dwell on land
Arise, and behold Atea above!
Let the farsighted who dwell on land
    Arise and see!
Look below in the presence of Te-tumu
At the jungles and rushing streams,
At the fountains of the deep,
At the fountains of the surface,
At the waves of the east,
At the waves of the west,
At the stable corners, at the burning corners,
At the great development over the eight directions.

Warrior's taunting song

Clap hands on thighs,
Rush headlong like an angry hog!
I do not flinch at a fly.

A whirlwind is anger, O Te-aho-roa,
A rock breaker is anger,
A strong north wind is anger
Which blows away grass sheaths.

Give me the fearless warrior
With rage and endurance.
This is I, Huriaau.
My father was a greater warrior than yours.
You cannot lift my spear.

Song of Pa'ea

Pa'ea is a place name meaning wall-of-escape. The yellow sea reflects the yellow rays of the sun.

Let the great standing river
Wall in its small-leafed ava.
Tell it with the trumpet and drum,
Wall in the ava upon Mount Mahu-ta'a.
O rain of the rocks,
Conceal your fish
That go to the deeps of the long bonito!
Go for parakeet feathers to Ra'iatea,
To distinguish the handsome warrior
Wearing the gardenia of Tupai
Blended with the red feathers of Rarotonga,
Deal kindly with the mountaineers.
It is the great black Utu-ai mist
Of the wall of the yellow sea,
Of the land that Hiro splashed.
When the parakeet gods are caught with gum
Beware! Beware!

Invocation for fire-walking

You who caused the fire in the fire pit—
Put it out!
O dark earthworm, O shining earthworm!
Fresh water, sea water!
Heat of the fire, red of the fire!
Help the feet of the walkers,
Cool the heat of the stones!
O you cold beings,
Let us pass through the middle of the fire pit!
O Great-woman-who-tends-fire-in-the-skies,
Hold tight the leaves
That fan away the fire—
Let us go through the fire pit!

A chief's refusal

I will not give her up! Why should I give her up—
I, Teuraiterai of the six skies! the Ura that clings to
    my eyes!
The Ura, sunshine from Raratoa, my dear treasure.
One king lulled to sleep his dear Ura.
Like two united, I should die without her.
Tie up the heavens like a net.
Tangle the clouds of the sky, the clouds of Pua.
Open the net, make me dry.
Dry the thousand thousand bonds that unite us.
The net, the net holds well.

A chief's lament for home

From Mataoae I look toward my land, Tetianina,
The mountain Tearatapu, the valley Temaite,
My drove of pigs on Mourahi, the great mountain.
Mist hides the mountain.
My cloak is spread.
Oh that the rain clear
That I may see the great mountain!
Aue! the wall of Mapuhi, dear land of mine.

The drums that sound above Fareura
Draw the winds of the south to me
For a fan to fan the chief Aromaiterai.
I long for the sight of my home.

The Tuamotus

Creation chant

Life appears in the world,
Life springs up in Hawaiki.
The Source-of-night sleeps below
    in the void of the world;
    in the taking form of the world,
    in the growth of the world,
    the life of the world,
    the leafing of the world,
    the unfolding of the world,
    the darkening of the world,
    the branching of the world,
    the bending down of the world.
Waves swerve aside,
With the tide rising inland,
With the tide rising seaward.
The tide rises till it touches Atea,
A sea below
    in the narrowness, in the confinement;
    in this, in that.
That gods may appear,
That people may issue forth—
Atea produces above,
Fakahotu produces below,
Through whom life was born into the world.

Greeting of Tane

Hail my chief, Tane!
There is not a god traveling the region of the skies,
Only one, Tane!
> Tane thundering on the land,
> Tane thundering in the skies,
> Tane the thunderer,
> Tane the cloud,
> Tane standing at the temple,
> Tane standing within,
> Tane the braider,
> Tane the torch bearer,
> Tane with blood inspiring sympathy, that he be
>   given sympathy by Rongo and Tutavake.

He is the beloved one, the teacher of chiefs,
The whirlwind on the land,
The crimson of the sky,
The glowing red of the sky,
The scarlet of the sky,
The clearness of the sky.
It is the sacred sky of Tane.
Tane here is the supreme ruler of the skies.
Hail to Tane!
It is the highest acclaim!
He is the trumpet, the drum, the leaves of kava,
The maker of chiefs.
Come forth,
Emerge encircled by the rainbow, with the flashing of
    lightning in the sky, with the crowding round of
    the multitude!
Hail to the chief,
Hail to the ancestor of chiefs!

Farewell to my land

From the legend of the demigod Rata, who built a great canoe in which he went to seek his lost parents.

O my land standing forth!
Hide your face,
Be lost, lost to sight in the voyage.
Let me be lost in launching away from land
With the temple;
Let my land standing out be lost!
Hide your face as I say farewell;
And bid me conceal,
Hide my feelings as I say goodbye,
Say goodbye to the woods of my land
    Till another time.

Rata's lament for his father

This lament is chanted by two voices; the first presents the first line of each stanza and the second the second line. The chorus chants the rest of the stanza.

1

O tropic bird of remote seas braving the fury of the storm,
Mount on beating wings as you launch into flight!
    O, speed onward to the shore, seeking the hidden dwellers of the land,
    Sweep out to sea, seeking the hidden dwellers of the deep!
    A father—

2

The father has long vanished into the place of the dead.
Mount on beating wings as you flash into flight!
    O, speed onward to the shore, seeking the hidden dwellers of the land,
    Sweep out to sea, seeking the hidden dwellers of the deep!
    Alas for the father—dead in the dark pit.
    Where can the lost father be?

Chant to announce a catch of turtle

"The foundation of Tongareva" is a term applied to the bottom of the sea where the turtle hides. "A plover without feathers" signifies the man who brings the news. Matariki is the name for a female turtle.

Intone the chant to announce a catch!
Tiriri, tiriri,
Tarara, tarara!
Let it be a clinging girdle, a hanging girdle,
Wrap round, wrap round the girdle of Tu!
That is the girdle through which was uncovered,
    brought to view,
The foundation of Tongareva,
As a large coral, a shelf of soft coral, a hard limestone
    rock.
That bird above flaps its wings,
A plover without feathers.
So-and-so is the person by whom this turtle was
    taken—
A great fish, a fish taken on the grapple,
Grappled by my mighty hook presided over by
    Ruahatu.
Thus is flung down
The broken flipper of Matariki.

Prayer offering turtle flesh to the gods

The victim is tied,
The turtle is tied up.
The tern twitters, the gray-back tern from Hiti.
From the god Tamarua of Hiti,
Shadow of the god, carry off the food!
Here comes the flesh of turtle,
For you, gods,
Eat!
Gods who stay, gods who wander,
Tara, Kaipoa, Varoa, Te Ariki-putai, Haroa-mai-
    to-ragi;
Muna-iti, Munariki;
There is the flesh of turtle,
For you, gods,
Eat!
It is beside you, there in the nether world,
Now it is free of restrictions!
Take it!

Prayer for arrival of turtle at the temple

Tira means the mast of a ship but is used here as a symbol of the phallus.

1

Where is my tira?
My tira comes running.
Where is my tira?
My tira gleams,
My tira inquires.
Now the procreant power of Ruahatu is loosed
That it reach the ocean,
That it be thronged.
Exalt the ocean!

2

The sea is covered with great waves, the sea is
    whipped by winds,
The sea is beaten down by the storm.
Now the procreant power of Ruahatu is loosed
That it reach the ocean,
That it be thronged with fish.
Exalt the ocean!

Chant for Horahora

Chanted by two alternating voices and a chorus. The name of the sacred temple, Mata-aru-ahau, means first wooing. The name of the field, Nuku-roa, means long thrusts.

Takaki is the lover
Takaki is the lover
Horahora is the maiden.
You two shall live together within the sacred temple,
    Mata-aru-ahau.

Ho, the sacred temple!
There shall sleep—
There you shall sleep together
Within the sacred enclosure of the temple.

Takaki shall kneel over the maiden on the field of
    Nuku-roa.
Ho, the sacred field of strife!
A radiant princess,
A radiant princess is the maiden.
Horahora gives herself to her lover
In the land of swirling flame.
The sap of maidenhead flows.

Shall dwell together—
You two shall dwell together
Within Ahu-tu, house of the gods
Until the day when wind breaks the sea surface.
Until the lover departs—
Horahora remains behind.

    EPILOGUE
You shall dwell in the night realm of Kiho,
The last place of repose.

Chant of Kororupo

Kororupo is the entrance to the realm of death.

The portal of Kororupo—
Stretch your hand within, extend your groping
    hand—
        My soul is a wild pigeon—
        A petrel, a stormy petrel!
The far journey is bitter cold.
You are gatekeeper at the portal of Havaiki—
        A pigeon, a wild pigeon,
        My soul is a wild pigeon!
A sandpiper twittering at the portal of Kororupo.
Uttering a plaintive note, suddenly my soul starts
    up—
        The soul—it is the soul!
There beside you lingers the spirit, like a bird
    pausing at the Gate of Havaiki.
Chilled by the cold wind it begins to ruffle its
    feathers, to spread them out—
        My soul going its long way here!
A heron, uttering its mournful cry at the portal of
    Kororupo,
Over and over and over repeating its night cry—
        A pigeon, a wild pigeon!
Speed to the sky above, to the dawn, to the world of
    light!

The Marquesas

Chant honoring a first-born son

A covering of mist shrouds Mount Feani,
The cloud is a waist cloth for Matia,
Sacred is the cloud,
A wreath of smoke for the chief.
A covering of mist shrouds Teheia,
The cloud is the waist cloth of A'o Tona,
Sacred is the cloud,
A wreath of smoke for the chief,
A wreath of smoke for the handsome youth.
Here, with her hair handsomely done up,
Is his mother, Viipohutu—it is her song!

Love song

By Moa Tetua, a blind leper. He sings about the love affairs of his son Piu. A sudden change from third to first person is a common device.

The dream image fades away, the dream of the red
    pandanus keys
Strung with ti leaves in a fine rain!
He is a handsome garland.
Brave is Tahia's mouth, but her eyes tremble at the
    spring, Hoa-tuki,
Desiring the boy from the valley.
A precious fan of dotted feathers,
A piece of loincloth were given as a brave husband's
    token of love.
Come, seek a fruit!
Hold your breath!
Pressed close to my lover in the mountain,
We hide away like children, my lover and I,
Until the shadows of the sun conceal the summit of
    Fe'ani mountain.
The kava leaves are lifted high toward me!
Climb the high pukatea tree, break off, O Piu,
The branch of the precious treasure of Atea.
Swing over the precipice called Flowers-at-the-
    mountain-peak.
The time with Ti'ahe'e-e-fatu.
My garland makes my lover happy.
Lightning flashes on the flowers of great Tonai'e
    mountain,
Like my eyes beckoning

To sleep in shame
In the house of songs at Fiti-nui.
It is the first time your eyes have seen the lovely ripe
    breadfruit.
I saw you before when you were tapu.
When I mated with the chief the sun was hot,
You were chiefly, you were handsome!
You came along Akaka stream.
My soul and lover, my palm leaf,
My shiny leaf, farewell Piu!
My robe is wet with tears,
And my nose swollen at being left alone!
With you on the silent Motu-tapu!

Be careful
By Moa Tetua

Be careful lest the day come when you are old,
And old, you leave behind the garlands and love-
    making.
You are despised, you are separated from Uriha.
The sky is darkened for the lover.
I dance in grief for the death of Vini,
For him I wound myself!
Who has foolishly taken my earrings,
Dripping with the rain of tears as I turn?
Like a reflection in the water, through tears I see you
    leave . . .
I turn my head,
My head is in a shadow near a flower standing high.
I, Fau-ti'i-kohea, have come
To the clean cave . . . of Ha'apape.
Pandanus garlands are cast away . . . the day I leave
    for O'ova'u.
Uri of Anamea wept.
Love is cared for tenderly and presses deep
    within me.
Do you forget us,
Two straying sweethearts from Puanea,
The day we were lost in the strange grotto
And the moon was new?
Such was my real food;
When my husband was separated from me
There was only hunger . . .

Hiva'oa balances

By M'u. Hiva'oa is an island in the Marquesas. The flower wreath alludes to a lover.

Hiva'oa balances like a dancing flower-leaf
As our canoe turns back,
Sailing like a bird in flight!
Swiftly the sun has fled, behold, it is night!
Shadows lengthen on the channel
Like wind-tossed flowers.
Ti'i gives a garland and a feast and a dance,
Singing and dancing until dawn whitens the heavens.
I sigh for my wreath of sweet flowers!
My wreath is perhaps torn,
My wreath of sweet flowers!
Pretty as a fruit-plucking pole harvesting perfume as
    food
Torn to shreds!
Torn to shreds, my garland of sweet flowers!
Beauty is torn to shreds!

The faufe'e bird

By Puko'i. The girls who sing this song imitate the flight of birds, the stormy sea, the rain, wind and thunder. The ku'a is a red parakeet. Its feathers are highly prized.

The faufe'e flies in the sunlight, wings motionless.
The tempestuous booby dives into the waters.
The wild pigeon and the ku'a claw
In changing sea and rain and hot sunshine,
In thunder through the mists.
The northeast wind strikes—
Madly I dart away!
Faster fly the birds!
Faster sings the song!
Faster fly the birds!
Birds in the clouds! Birds in the mists!
Song of clouds, song of mists!
My fledgling flies to Fatu'uku,
Flies straight into my famous song,
Wings spread!

Strong fires disturb
By Tamau

1

Strong fires disturb the girl, she is mad with love.
My thoughts are sad, they are in the cruel mists and
    mountains.
I weep as I make my clothes and sing my song.
Why has he gone?
    REFRAIN
I wear a garland and grasp the hand of my beloved,
    Little Kuʻa.
Dewdrops are in my song, dewdrops.
A gift of a wreath, a wreath of peace.

2

I wrap my body
In the mists of a night cooled by the west wind.
Gentle is the path of the northeast wind.
We go to the flowers of the plumeria tree,
By the spring we wreathe our garlands,
For he and I are together.

3

I wear a garland of seven-petaled flowers.
The mountains are our love,
And the sky our clothing,
And wreaths our destruction.

When a man's body is young

By Kahuʻeinui Barsinas

1

When a man's body is young,
At night he gives up his sleep
And sings, and sings!

2

When love sickness comes,
The singing sickness,
This is the dizzy sickness,
Even the earth and clouds are consumed with desire!

CHORUS

Until the body is like an old woman,
Like an eel in a hole in the sea,
Pounding, pounding!

Easter Island

A chant of creation

God-of-angry-look by lying with Roundness made the
    poporo berry.
Himahima marao by lying with Lichen-in-the-soil
    made the lichen,
Parent-mother by lying with Pipiri hai tau made
    wood,
Ti by lying with Tattooing made the ti plant,
Elevation by doing it with Height made the inland
    grass.
Sharpness by lying with Adze produced obsidian,
Twining by lying with Beautiful-face-with-
    penetrating-tongue produced the morning glory,
Parent-god by lying with Angry-eel produced the
    coconut,
Grove by doing it with Trunk produced the ashwood.
Veke by lying with Water-beetle made the dragonfly,
Stinging-fly by doing it with Swarm-of-flies produced
    the fly,
Branch by lying with Fork-of-tree made Beetle-that-
    lives-in-rotten-wood,
Lizard-woman by lying with Whiteness made the
    gannet.
Hard-soil by lying with Covering-below made the
    sugar cane.
Bitterness by doing it with Bad-taste produced the
    kape,
Tail by lying with Hina oio produced the crayfish,
Killing by doing it with Stingray made the shark.
Tiki-the-chief by lying with Heap-of-earth made Hina
    kauhara;

Kuhikia by lying with Wetness made the bulrush;
Kuhikia by lying with Pigeon made the seagull;
Small-thing by doing it with Imperceptible-thing
   made the fine dust in the air.
      It runs red, the blood of kovare.
      Abundant the kovare, rough the eels.
      The rain falls in long drops.

A prayer for rain

A fragment.

O rain, long tears of Hiro,
You fall down,
You beat down,
O rain, long tears of Hiro.

Dampened by dew

A Miru girl, leaving her lover in the morning, is dampened with dew.

O Miru, you are dampened to the bones by dew
By the dew of the Rano-aroi.
You won't be dry when you go
To soak the paper mulberry
To make the cloth for the ribbon of your topknot.

Love song

Sung by a girl whose younger sister loves the same man she does.

O Mea, for your body both the little one and the big
    one are fighting.
It is winter, my friend, the flower is very fragrant,
The flower is very fragrant.
It is summer, the flower, my friend,
Is withered on my breast, alas, alas.
The older wife is afraid.
Here is the wreath to hang an ornament,
The ornament is your face.
O my brother, O Mea.

You are sick with love

The girl is compared to a fish. The fins are her topknot.

You are sick with love
You are a crab that lives below at Ahu Akurenga.
You are a fish with topknot.
You go down,
O fish, you are my girl friend.
For a toro-miro tree that cannot break,
Seaweed of the parent separated by
The long rock.

O Manu

A married girl, shut in the house of her father-in-law,
wants to escape to meet her lover.

O Manu, my blood oozes
When I dig under the house, O Manu.
I do not eat the sweet potatoes
Of this old man, Maea-te-renga.

Mangareva

Tahaki's drum

From the legend of the demigod Tahaki, who had a beautiful red skin. The skin was stolen. In this poem he returns from the underworld where he retrieved the skin. His cousin Kirihi betrayed him, and Tahaki's drum reflects the doubt and confusion of Kirihi while the two journey home.

REFRAIN
Drum so softly sounding, causing wonder,
Drum that sounds so secretly,
I have bedecked myself
With beautiful flowers,
But yet one wonders.

1

Let us go on the rising tide,
Doubt rises with the breaking waves.
The drum now sounding belongs to the younger
    cousin,
And the elder is in doubt.

2

With Tahaki was the drum,
With Kirihi was the scouting of the way in doubt.

3

Kirihi, move over
Toward the first night-world,
To the first night-world,
Where doubt exists.

4
To the first night-world
Where the woman planned
To remove the eyes of Kirihi,
Whom she doubted.

Song of departure

From the legend of Tahaki. Tahaki leaves Nua, his lover, and she sings this song. His back is a symbol of his leaving her.

    REFRAIN
The body of the loved one
    warmed the back
Of the chiefly lover who was
    loved so well.

    1

Tahaki has arrived
    beside the green tree, alas.

    2

Tahaki has arrived
    beside the tree of farewell, alas.

The message of the frigate bird

A mother asks the bird for news of her son. She interprets the lowering of the feet and the bending of the beak to mean that he is dead.

REFRAIN
O son, O son of mine,
    O son!

1

Listen, O bird
    that flies up above,
Have you seen
    my beloved son dead
Who stayed among
    the myriads of Tahiti?
Feathers on your legs
Feathers on your wings,
Your beak bends low.
O son!

2

As a torea bird were you
    flitting along the shore
On the coast of distant Tahiti?
O son!

3

The canoe I provided
In which my son embarked,
The son so dear to me,
Cast up on a distant land.
O son!

4

You are a moon
That will not rise again.
O son, O son of mine,
    O son!
The chill dawn breaks without you,
O son, O son of mine,
    O son!

The rich and the poor

From the folktale of Toga. In this poem Toga, whose father lives in Po, the other world, sits with a rich young man at a beauty show.

REFRAIN

The well-beloved has been rejected,
So I shall hurry far
Beyond to my mother, alas!
The well-beloved has been rejected.

1

Sit on the high stone seat,
Sit with high-held head,
The one with a wealthy father.

2

Put on the feathered headdress,
Sit with haughty glancing eyes,
The one with a wealthy father.

3

Hang round your neck the ivory jewel,
Sit with proudly heaving breast,
The one with a wealthy father.

4

Grasp in your hand the chiefly staff,
Sit with imposing dignity,
The one with a wealthy father.

5

Gird round your waist the barkcloth kilt,
Sit with chiefly arrogance,
The one with a wealthy father.

6

Sit on the corner of the low house platform,
sit with downcast head,
The one with a father in poverty.

7

Hold in your hand the menial staff,
Sit with drooping shoulders,
The one with a father in poverty.

8

Tie round your loins the ti-leaf kilt,
Sit with shame-bent back,
The one with a father in poverty.

The flower at the spring

From the folktale of Toga. Toga has climbed a tree hanging over a pool. His former wife, Ugaru, comes to draw water and sees the reflection of Toga. She uses a love name for him, Matahara.

REFRAIN
Ah, we two! Here are we two,
    Ugaru-te-ganagana and I,
We two were united in love,
We two!
Let us climb up to pick flowers,
We two!

1

Beside the spring,
I peered down,
You peered down,
We saw the image
    of Matahara, the beloved.
Ah, we two!

2

Peering down I saw
The reflection of the water bottle,
The image of Matahara, the beloved.
Ah, we two!

Joy turns to sadness

From the folktale of Toga. The poem tells of the meeting and final parting of Toga and his former wife, Ugaru.

REFRAIN
Joy turns to sadness.

1

I stretched out my hand,
    O my beloved,
It touched below your waist,
Ah, joy will turn to sadness.

2

I stretched out my hand,
    O my beloved,
It touched your sweetness,
Ah, joy will turn to sadness.

3

I stretched out my hand,
    O my beloved,
It fell into empty space,
Ah, joy has turned to sadness.

Sea burial of Toga's daughter

From the folktale of Toga.

REFRAIN
I lowered you down.

1

You have been lowered down to the deep,
Down to the depths, my loved one,
And I lowered you down.

2

Our daughter, the Princess who
    plaited precious things,
She died on the open sea.
My darling, I lowered you down.

3

A deep-sea fisherman I,
Storm-bound at night,
But the way was too long
For the gods to hear,
So your body, my dear one,
I lowered you down.

The sacred house

From a legend. Uru warned his dauther and her husband
not to enter his sacred house. But they do.

    REFRAIN
O loved ones!
O cherished wife,
O beloved husband,
O dear ones!
Out of a clear sky
Lightly falls the rain,
Lightly drizzles down
    the rain of Heagi-kura.
O my loved ones!

    1

I command you two,
You two must not enter
    into my house, a sacred house,
A sacred house dwelt in
    by a priest, by me.

    2

I will reach up with my hands
To draw down the heavy
    drops of rain from Heagi-kura.

The casting out of love

REFRAIN
The love for you that gnaws within my breast,
The casting out progresses now,
    cast out, cast out,
That I forever may forget you.

    1

The love is now torn out
    that once I felt for you.

    2

Dear one, I die
    beneath the waves that sweep over me.

I am left alone

REFRAIN
Beloved, I am left alone,
O Te Matererea, my dear one,
The odor of the death of the beloved
    assails me,
I am left alone.

    1

The waves flow over you,
The waves recede,
The waves lift up your body,
The waves wash Te Matererea.
I am left alone.

    2

You were borne in
By the waves of Pua-ragahia.
Now we two are parted,
O beloved, I am left alone.
Washed up on the strand was
    the precious one of Aiuragi.
O beloved, I am left alone.

Lament

A human husband laments for a wife taken by a non-human husband.

REFRAIN

Spreading to seaward of Putatai-roa,
O Te Tepeiru, fear spreads abroad,
Because you are dead.

1

O Te Tepeiru, alas,
My princess who departed so soon.

2

What is the evil thing
that spreads fear abroad?

3

Fear of a cruel lover,
That is the evil thing that causes fear.

4

The hand of the cruel lover,
That is the cruel thing that causes fear.

5

The blood shed by an evil lover,
That is the cruel cause that
    spreads fear abroad.

The canoe of Mamau-ora

From a story. Mamau-ora was killed in her canoe by two evil nephews.

REFRAIN
The wind arises, the wind arises,
The waves from the south are calmed,
The waves from the north are calmed.
The wind arises!

1

From where returned
    the canoe of Mamau-ora?

2

From sailing in the west wind
    returned the canoe of Mamau-ora.

3

From the beach where small nuts grew
    returned the canoe of Mamau-ora.

4

From the far distant beach
    returned the canoe of Mamau-ora.

Haul away

This poem speaks of a defeated people hurriedly putting their canoe in the water to escape the enemy.

    REFRAIN
Haul away, haul, haul away,
Danger is near,
Fear of the enemy,
So haul away, haul, haul away.

    1

What is the wind
    that brings the big seas?

    2

The north wind is the wind
    that brings the huge waves.

    3

The northwest wind is the wind
    that brings the great seas.

    4

The west wind is the wind
    that brings the rough storms.

Song of things in the upper world

A woman, Meiraga, was taken to the underworld. Her husband, Tako, went after her. On their return to the upper world, women along the way asked Meiraga what things in the upper world she had yearned for.

REFRAIN

The beloved sincerely mourned for
By a thousand thoughts of former days,
I weep for love of you,
O beloved, mourned for indeed.

1

O Meiraga the beloved, what is the thing
That you weep for
In the far-off upper world?

The leafy freshness of my land of Taupapa—
A somber picture from the realm above.

2

O Meiraga the beloved, what is the thing
That you weep for
In the far-off upper world?

The green fresh leaves of taro growing at Te Puna-nui-a-tauga,
A haunting picture from the world above.

3
O Meiraga the beloved, what is the thing
That you weep for
In the far-off upper world?

The firm straight stalks of taro planted at Tutuira,
A yearned-for picture of the land above.

4
O Meiraga the beloved, what is the thing
That you weep for
In the far-off upper world?

The full sweet tubers of taro harvested at
    Te Matavarivari,
A distressing picture from the home above.

Lament for old age

    REFRAIN
Alas! We grow old, O beloved,
We two.

    1

We two indeed together, O beloved,
When we two were little
When we played together in the sea.

    2

We two indeed together, O beloved,
When we took our walks together
As we were growing up.

    3

We two indeed together, O beloved,
When your breasts were firm and round,
When your breasts drooped in motherhood.

    4

We two indeed together, O beloved,
When your hair floated down your back,
When your body was strong and virile.

    5

We two indeed together, O beloved,
When our bodies grew old and thin,
Like a flatfish resting on the bottom.

            6
We two indeed together, O beloved,
When so feeble we but sat apart,
So feeble we could but rest the hours away.

            7
We two indeed together, O beloved,
When our dim eyes gaze at the misty skies,
When vision fails to see their splendor.
Ah, where does God draw me?

Cook Islands

Prayer over a human sacrifice to Rongo

Fragment of an ancient chant.

    Stately, noble priest!
Sweet peace, welcome offering!
Securely fastened and well-tied,
These human hands and human form
Dedicated to this fate by the gods:
Doomed to sacrifice by the god Rongo.

Great Vātea is the guardian of the ocean.
    It is ruffled by him:
    It is calmed by him.

Here is ironwood of noble growth—
    A graceful tree,
    With numerous branches.
    Cut down this ironwood tree;
    Divide its trunk;
    Split it with wedges,
    For the making of spears.

In every age the ironwood has provided
    Death-dealing spears
    For the use of warriors only—
    From time immemorial.

And bravely have we wielded them!
The wild ti root of the hills was our food,
But now we shall enjoy plenty.
We rejoice on this day.

Lately we hid in the rocks—
The refuge of the conquered.
But now we shall enjoy plenty,
We rejoice on this day.

Where has she gone?

Composed by Naupata in memory of his wife. Avaiki is the land of the dead. The song is performed by a solo voice and chorus alternating.

Where has she gone?

She has gone to Avaiki,
She disappeared at the edge of the horizon
Where the sun drops through.
We weep for you.

Yes, I will forever weep
And continuously seek for you.

I shed bitter tears—
I weep for the lost wife of my bosom.
Alas! You will not return.

Oh, that you would return!

Come back to this world,
Return to my embrace.
You are like a branch torn off by the storm.

Torn off, and now in Avaiki—
That distant land to which you fled.

Puvai leading a band of ghosts to the underworld

By Iikura, ca. 1795. This poem was chanted by alternating chorus and solo voices.

INTRODUCTION

A favoring breeze sweeps the entrance of the ghost
    cave;
It is for Puvai about to depart.
Lightly he skims over the crest of the waves.

FOUNDATION

Farewell, beloved parents!
Let a mourning procession follow
Over the rugged shore of the south.
Weep for a son of such tender nature
Before a fair wind carries me to spirit-land.

I

A favoring breeze sweeps the entrance
Of the ghost cave Anakura.
Listen to the hum of the ghosts.
It is the hum of spirits passing over rocks,
Crowding along the beach by Double Cave.

He is about to depart.
Lightly he skims over the crest of the waves.

2

There is the canoe of Puvai.
He bends sorrowfully over it.
Yes, very sorrowfully he bends over it.
Take your seat in front, son,
Clothed in ghostly network;
Turn your face to the other land.

He is about to depart.
Lightly he skims over the crest of the waves.

3

Let the southwest wind ruffle the sea.
Awake, northwest wind.
Tiki, sister of Veʻetini, leads the way.
Mangaia fades from the sight of Puvai,
Driven away by the violence of winds.

He is about to depart.
Lightly he skims over the crest of the waves.

4

Beloved child of Motuone—
Of Motuone, your weeping mother,
Glance tenderly back on the hills
And mountains of the interior.
Come back to the fair valley of Tamarua,
The place where you were born.

He is about to depart.
Lightly he skims over the crest of the waves.

Ai e ruaoo ē! E rangai ē!

Death lament for Varenga

By Koroa, ca. 1817. "Sun-rising" refers to the ancient home of the tribe. Miru is the ugly spirit of the underworld.

INTRODUCTION

Varenga who came from the Sun-rising
Is now wed in spirit-land.
She was wooed by a shadow.
Such was my dream on the mountain.

FOUNDATION

My dream was of you at the Sun-rising—
Your form dazzling as lightning.
You were watching for the dawn
When I awoke from my sleep
On the steep mountain side.

I

Varenga who came from the Sun-rising;
    Yes, my Varenga!
Miru will cherish you in your maidenhood—
    Your lovely maidenhood!
In life you were admired by all
Wherever your light steps wandered.
Now you are wooed by a shadow.
Such was my dream on the mountain.

2

You were buried in the ancestral marae
On the side of steep Maungaroa,
Hidden by the tall fern—
Yes, hidden by the tall fern.
Perhaps your spirit is revisiting the spot,
Hovering among the wild rocks.
Now you are wooed by a shadow.
Such was my dream on the mountain.

3

Your house in the west is decayed,
Your house at the gathering place of ghosts,
Built by your ancestors where spirits
Rest awhile and chatter in the evening
Or wander about at the edge of the cliffs
Or sit on the stones gazing at the interior.
Now you are wooed by a shadow.
Such was my dream on the mountain.

Ai e ruaoo ē! E rangai ē!

Tuvalu

Vaitupu songs

1

I walked along the eastern shore
Round the outskirts of Sapepe
Your footprints are hard to forget.

2

I stand at Fangamotu
I watch the dawn breaking
Breaking over the mid-lagoon
I decide to sleep
But I remain awake
My eyes remain open!

3

Birds sing among the puka trees
To converse with me
Ho! you there!
I shall seek a mate on my accustomed path
Oh! my accustomed love-sick path.

Kapingamarangi

The post standing in the sky

The post which stands in space;
Insert it.
May it be held firmly below.

Love song

I was lying in my house
When I thought of you.
I stood up, went out to find you.
I saw the place where you sleep.
I crouched toward you in pitch darkness.
I am not afraid because of my love for you.
The premna tree leaf trembles, flashes,
Then you know it is I.

I go down to the lagoon

I go down to the lagoon,
Steer my canoe straight to the reef.
A trigger fish speeds by.
I dive, go off, swim.
My back is hot.
I continue on, continue on, feeling fine.
The rigging is tight, well secured,
Speeding on, sailing on, quivering;
Sailing on, sailing on, returning!

I am on the water
By Timoweti

I am on the water, poling.
This canoe exists to carry us sailing.
When the wind blows, who will see you?
That will be known when the sail appears and gleams
    against the opening between the islets.
Chanting is heard on the islets,
As it was heard from the earliest times.
When the shallows of Hangaeha are reached
The tide in the pass is high.
We land, turn, go out again, paddle on the lagoon.
As the tide has come in, make your line ready
    quickly.
See if those who have arrived
Are rapidly pulling in their lines to the canoes.
Give bait so that a hand can cast it.
There it goes!
The kina fish smile as they wander from piece to
    piece.

Chant for the bonito canoe

by Timoweti and Korowe

He awoke in the lonely house standing at the border
    of the land; he lifted his canoe,
Turned his canoe Hikumeruti, headed for the islets
    south.
Entered a branch of the pass and appeared paddling
    westward.
Birds, noddy terns, fed alone, appearing below the
    sky.
He stayed on his three-legged stool. As the birds
    moved, he trailed his hook.
He cast it in the foam of his wake.
A fish struck while waiting for the Pleiades.
His pole bends, cracks, breaks on the sacred ocean
    here.
The stick of Utamatua is broken, chant to the ocean!
"May the god rest" he says to the tail of his bonito.
    The news spread.
You all paddled your canoe until close to the
    breakers,
Then you saw and spoke truthfully when you were
    before the people.
Just carry up the canoe.

Search for

This chant and the following one were recited at the time of a fishing ritual when a basket of coconuts was offered in a sacred place.

Turn, turn, search for;
Carry to the children.
I walk carefully
With the basket to the children, you.
Sacred power is there, the coconuts are there, the
    nuts are there.
The basket containing the coconuts is there pointed
    toward you.
This will bring sacred power.
The light travels, flames, goes forth.
Flames, goes forth.

The man stayed

The man stayed on the promontory
Waiting for the sun to rise.
When it was bright, I picked up my paddle
Then looked at my food, the bonito coming here.
Then I went out on the ocean
Then I wished I had stayed ashore
Pulling up sea urchins on the reef,
Just by the reef.

Tikopia

Lament for a friend

My paddle from the stern of the canoe
My paddle from the bow
Has slipped away
Buried beneath far skies!
Now if it had slipped away at sea
That you might sleep in sweet burial—

The unclasping of our hands
Friend!
But to be buried in the earth
Indeed you have parted from the crew.

Dream song

The dead man appears to the canoe owner in a dream and bewails his fate.

Turn your stern to me
Turn your stern to me
But the fish went in the path
Of the ocean.

My swimming, my long swimming
In the ocean wastes
My body nuzzled by the grey birds.

New Zealand

Creation chant

Io dwelt within breathing-space of immensity.
The universe was in darkness, with water everywhere.
There was no glimmer of dawn, no clearness, no
    light.
And he began by saying these words,
That he might cease remaining inactive.
    "Darkness, become a light-possessing darkness."
And at once light appeared.
He then repeated those self-same words in this
    manner,
That he might cease remaining inactive,
    "Light, become a darkness-possessing light."
And again intense darkness supervened.
Then a third time he spoke, saying,
    "Let there be a darkness above,
    Let there be darkness below.
    Let there be darkness to Tupua,
    Let there be darkness to Tawhito;
    It is a darkness overcome and dispelled.
    Let there be one light above,
    Let there be one light below.
    Let there be light to Tupua,
    Let there be light to Tawhito.
    A dominion of light,
    A bright light."
And now a great light prevailed.
Io then looked to the waters which encompassed him,
    and spoke a fourth time, saying,

"You waters of Tai-kama, be separate.
Heaven be formed."
Then the sky became suspended.
"Bring forth Tupu-koro-nuku."
And at once the moving earth lay stretched
abroad . . .

Creation chant

In the beginning was the 'Night',
The 'Night' begot the 'Light',
The 'Light' begot the 'Light standing long',
The 'Light long standing' begot 'Nothingness',
The 'Nothingness' begot 'Nothingness the possessed',
The 'Nothingness the possessed' begot 'Nothingness
    the made excellent',
The 'Nothingness the made excellent' begot
    'Nothingness the fast bound',
The 'Nothingness the fast bound' begot
    'Nothingness the first',
The 'Nothingness the first' begot 'Moisture',
'Moisture' married 'The strait, the vast, the clear',
And their progeny were Rangi, the heaven, and Papa,
    the earth.

Creation chant

The first period: of Thought
>   From the conception the increase,
>   From the increase the thought,
>   From the thought the remembrance,
>   From the remembrance the consciousness,
>   From the consciousness the desire.

The second period: of Darkness
>   The knowledge became fruitful;
>   It dwelt with the feeble glimmering;
>   It brought forth night:
>   The great night, the long night,
>   The lowest night, the loftiest night,
>   The thick night, the night to be felt;
>   The night to be touched,
>   The night not to be seen,
>   The night of death.

The third period: of Light
>   From the nothing the begetting,
>   From the nothing the increase,
>   From the nothing the abundance,
>   The power of increasing,
>   The living breath;
>   It dwelt with the empty space, and produced the
>   atmosphere which is above us,
>   The atmosphere which floats above the earth.
>   The great firmament above us dwelt with the
>   early dawn,
>   And the moon sprang forth;

The atmosphere above us dwelt with the heat,
And then came the sun;
They were thrown up above, as the chief eyes of
   Heaven:
Then the Heavens became light,
The early dawn, the early day,
The mid-day. The blaze of day from the sky.

The fourth period: of Land
   The sky above dwelt with Havaiki,
   And produced lands:
   Taporapora,
   Tauwarenikau,
   Kukuparu,
   Wawau atea,
   Whiwhi te Rangiora
      . . .

The creation of woman

Ha! It leaps into life,
It is the first light,
It is bright morning,
Out of dawn comes the disciple.
The people of Hawaiki
Drawn in,
Like the clenching of a hand
On Hawaiki.
Crouched within,
Knees drawn up,
Tiki, the spring—
Hands, take shape.
Tiki, the source, the kneeling one—
Knees drawn up,
He weeps for his food,
And stretches
Bold Tiki!
Soft Tiki!
Red rain falls from the skies,
Open the great womb of the earth,
Come forth! It is the daughter!
The stranger, Hine-mana-hiri!

Chant for bailing a canoe

A chant for the Aotea canoe, which sailed in the great migration from Hawaiki to New Zealand in the fourteenth century. Tawhiri-matea is the god of gales and tempests. Tu-Raka-maomao is the god of ordinary winds.

I will uplift my bailer now,
The Ririno-o-te-rangi,
To the extreme limits of the heavens,
To the girdle of the heavens,
To the stability of the heavens,
To the resting place of heaven.
Adhere to the foundation of heaven,
Adhere to the summit of heaven,
Affix it to great heaven above,
The uprising, the uplifting,
The insertion, the bailing out
Of the water of my canoe.
Dry up to above,
Dry up to below,
Dry up to seaward,
To the great heaven above,
The bailer, the Tipua-horo-nuku.
There stands the deep blue ocean,
There stands the reddish ocean,
There stands the breaking ocean,
There stands the surging ocean,
There stands the ruddy shore.
Houra,

Dry up
The water of my canoe,
Houra,
Dry up,
Dry up that colored water
Of my canoe,
Houra,
Dry up
The sky of Tawhiri-matea at sea—
Of Tu-Raka-maomao.
Strike the prow of the canoe,
Dry up completely
The sea to Hawaiki.

Arrival at New Zealand

I arrive where an unknown earth is under my feet,
I arrive where a new sky is above me,
I arrive at this land
    A resting place for me.
O spirit of the earth! A stranger humbly offers his
    heart as food for thee.

From a lament for a son who burned to death

Hine-nui-te-po is death. Mahuika is the goddess of fire.

My ornamental ear-feather
Has long been misty from the fog.
My poor grieved heart
Is now aroused because of a curse
That was provoked.
Move off, until far away.
You were not left
At the altar of Paki-o-matiti,
Your skin was burning,
Scorched by the fire.
You must cover yourself
With taramea water
You must bathe
In the life-giving water of Tane
At Waipuna-atea.

Tide of Koroki
Crying and wailing
Sounding far off
Within Mangamaire
Stricken with the odor,
The patches of small mountain beech trees.
O departed son

Now within Pipiri
You were not covered
By the prized cloak,
By the winter night
So that your living spirit
Might return
In company to Wairau.
. . .
My greenstone neck ornament!
It is but that alone;
My prized ear-drop
Is severed from the ear,
My headdress of Tihauora,
Who repressed you.
Sleep on, O son,
You, the pillar of Aotea,
You must embark upon
The gentle-blown spirit canoe.
Your life oil then floats,
Resembling that of crushed titoki
To become an anointing
By the assembled low born.
Your near ones
Look downward.
My flock of sea terns
There, moving off,
Fill then
Your small stomach
With the food of the waters.

I see clearly
The path to the spirit world
There to be swallowed down

To Hine-nui-te-po.
I must share
In the fire of Mahuika
That singed and scorched
Your shriveled skin,
Your long straight hair
Burnt by the fire,
My son.

Prayer for victory in battle

Tu is the god of battle.

The heavens are clouded,
Cloud-covered.
It is heard here below,
    The thunder rolling,
It is heard here below,
    Echoing the expanse.

The quivering spear, surprise in flight,
Like the double-sided shark,
Is the fleetness of the footsteps,
Is the raging of the footsteps,
In blood are the footsteps,
Here the footsteps rush headlong.
It is the footsteps of Tu!
Stride over the stars!
Stride over the moon!
Flee! Take flight!
Now the death stroke.

Chant to incite warriors

This chant, from a legend, is sung by the woman, Apa-kura. The spider's web is a reference to the path of a god to the upper world.

Listen, stars! Hearken, O moon!
My arms and hands and feet
Shall wage a lasting war.
Wail the dirge of Apa-kura
To her elder kindred,
And wake the sleeping heart
To act, and satisfy revenge
For the death of him, Tu-whakararo.
Drink, drink deep of the bowls—
Those bowls kept on high.
In vain I try to climb
The spider's web; my path
Is less than nothing beneath my tread . . .

A war chant

The land is slipping away;
Where shall man find an abiding place?
O God of the underworld!
Hold fast our lands!
Bind, tightly bind!
Be firm, be firm
Nor let them be torn from our grasp.

Spiders, hide my face

Chant by a warrior who wants to remain hidden.

Spiders, hide my face;
Ants, obscure me from the foe;
O God of the underworld,
Come from your pit,
And let me enter it.
Search all around,
Gaze up and down,
See nothing but the empty land.

Te Rauparaha's farewell to Kawhia

Composed by Wharetiki, a warrior who had been taken prisoner. Before he was executed, he asked his captors to allow him to sing a song of farewell to his ancestral home, Kawhia. His father overheard and memorized the song. Te Rauparaha used the song for his farewell and substituted Honipaka for Kawhia. Te Kawau is a sea rock and Muriwhenua an undersea burial cave. The bird is the spirit of Te Rauparaha.

There flow the tides of Honipaka,
Now separated from me forever.
In spirit, I still cling to you.
And my aching heart
Grieves over that world apart
Which lies outspread above Te Motu Island.
Heedless of my painful fate,
O all you tribes that sleep
In the last long sleep,
A far-off tribute now I give.
The tides will still ebb and flow,
Flowing strongly, rising and leaping,
Until, leaping over Te Kawau at Muriwhenua
I see the waves rushing by!
See to my cherished bird,
It is distracted with grief;
And early, within the House of Mourning,
It will be hidden from my eyes.
This gentle breeze of summer
Brings the sound of wailing:

O you House of Mourning!
O you House of Ati Awa!
Lament, let the tears flow,
You shall indeed be a sepulchre
For this my song of sorrow,
    Alas!

Potatau's song of sorrow

Potatau was elected to the first kingship of the Maori. He was an old man who wished to live quietly and did not want to be king. He became king in 1859 and died in 1860.

Often these times, in pensive mood, I sit
With thoughts heaped up
Like entangled weeds:
My name now always on the lips of men—
Borne here and there with the winds that blow,
As if it were a passing jest on frivolous lips,
It is carried even to the distant South.
At Repanga, it is said, live two wise birds
Called Mumuhau and Takereto.
And here I am like them,
Pecked at and agitated by all the land.
Who will work and clear this weedy soil?
Look, I am now grey and worn with years;
The last horizon has moved up quite close;
Youthful, vigorous days are but a memory,
And my fretful soul is now at rest from all these.
Give me the life of women weaving,
As they gossip and children play around them,
Though my fame would then be enclosed
By the peaceful shores at Mauina.
It would indeed be a joy for me and mine:
You and I should not have heeded
The often-spoken seductive words,
Which, I think, will but lead to endless sorrow
For me . . . Alas, ah me!

Dirge for a chief

Alas, the bitter pain that gnaws within
For the wrecked canoe, for a friend who is lost.
My precious heron plume is cast on the ocean's shore,
And the lightning, flashing in the heavens,
Salutes the dead.

Where is authority in this world, since you have
    passed
By the slippery path, the sliding path to death?

Whakaahu Mountain stands alone in the distance,
For you are gone, the shelter of your people.
My bird that sang of ancient learning has flown,
The keel of Tainui, the plug of Aotea,
Now wailed by the women's flowing tears.
Your body lies beautiful in your dogskin tasseled
    cloak,
But your spirit has passed like a drifting cloud in the
    heavens.
All is well with you who lie in state on a chieftain's
    bier.
Ah, my precious green jade jewel, symbol of departed
    warriors!
The dragon emerged from his rocky fastness
And sleeps in the house of death.

A ritual spell

Light, light the holy fire
O Tiki, it burns on the sacred morning
Give us, O give us, O Tiki,
The sweetness of food; it burns,
Burns for thee, the juice of the pigeon,
Burns for thee, juice of the owl,
Burns for thee, juice of the parrot,
Burns for thee, juice of the fantail,
For thee, the sweetness of the eel
From what source?
From the spring where the sky turns red—
Give, let it be poured.

Vision

By Kaiteke. A priest invokes the gods to tell him by second sight his success.

What says the god of the night?
I will die at Mangawhai—
Never!
I will die in the ascent—
Never!
I will look on the place where the river
Opens out to the western sea—
Closed in, opened out—
At Waihi your harbor will be
Closed in.
The woman laughs, the war god
Tu will triumph, Tu
The war god
Tu will triumph, Tu
The war god.
The land breezes
Already blow another way.
Ah, I see the kahikatea trees
Standing over Kaiwaka, there, out there
Tu, the war god Tu
Hunts up and down
Up and down.
You are gods and they
Are small birds to be preserved
In potted fat
Forever.
Yes
Forever.

Song of mourning

By Matangi-Hauroa. For the Maori, the distinction between the dead and the living is not great. Death is the gate between the living and the dead of one family.

I lie in darkness, as the dead shades gather,
Feeling you here, at my side—
I turn to greet you, reach out to grasp
A world of nothing, no one, nowhere.
You passed like a shadow in the night—
Lie still, my aching heart.

Let the sharp blades gouge me.
Let the children see.
Take it, Whiro, blood, strength, spirit—
I walk the path of our fathers,
They speak well of the way you died,
Your courage cries to the empty skies.

You were caught in Whanganui's coils.
Remember, watch the son of Tuwhakairihau;
Beware, there are other sons of Rakamaomao there;
Motai's hundred sons lie in wait.
Walk their beaches, scorn them—
Your body lies here.

Your name will live
In this place
And perhaps here in this poor house of proverbs.

A charm: Is it the wind?

Is it the wind that strokes your skin?
Or perhaps it is desire, desire for the one
To whom you clung, with whom you slept,
Who held you,
Who shared your griefs.
Let the wind do his work
Bring this, my love, to you
So you turn in your sleep
And weep for when we were
As one together. Love comes
Like a spring from the earth.

Song of a second wife

By Matahira. Her husband married a young girl.

Within me, thrusting endlessly
Against the belly that betrayed me—
Swollen now like Wharerewa Hill—
There's a little thing that would see
If you are his father still.
Let the wind blow, let the river flow,
Am I cloud or water-weed to go where they go?
You were a god and I but a child,
Now having used me, you cast me aside,
This little thing I gave, you deride,
Am I worthless thus to be denied?
O the misery of a second wife,
For me a famine, for him a feast;
I, the host, was least,
While he, the guest, took most.
But when he turned from me
I burned the more fiercely—
O Mare, do not tease me—
This is your canoe, you launched it on the sea;
I long to go to you, and yet—
And yet—better men seek my bed.
I'll be more careful who comes in your stead,
Ears may flap, but nothing will be said.

The deserted girl's lament

With quivering limbs
And bowed head I weep,
And restlessly turn on
My lonely sleeping mat.

Once fondly I dreamed
Your love never would wane.
Ah me! it is dead;
But mine ceaselessly burns.

Swamp-stains on the feet
Are washed clean in the stream,
But the heart-stains of love
Forever remain.

A mourning song for Rangiaho

By Te Heuheu Herea for his wife

Many women call on me to sleep with them
But I'll have none so worthless and so wanton;
There is not one like Rangiaho, so soft to feel
Like a small, black eel.
I would hold her again—
Even the wood in which she lies;
But like the slender flax stem
She slides from the first to the second heaven
The mother of my children
Gone
Blown by the wind
Like the spume of a wave
Into the eye of the void.

A song of sickness
By Hine Tangikuku

Neap-tide and the ebbing days slide
From my side as I stand
Here beyond the land
I love. The open doors
Of Mihimarino call me no more.

Sing, cicada, for soon you will die,
And so must I;
The bitterns cry doleful death,
The parrot chokes on his last breath.

The morning star swims in the sky
To this shore, where I
Lie washed in a sea of pain,
Writhing like one insane.
Fever-drunk, drifting
Like pollen in a dream, sifting
Like seed, I am not what I seem.

I see myself, twisted sinew,
Wasted flesh; the body I once knew
Has no substance, unsustained,
Is itself the food of pain.
I am dead weed cast upon the shore.

Chant to restore breath to a dead person

Thy breath, my breath,
Open out, close up, thy breath,
Return inside then;
It enters; it is sacred;
It flays, it strikes;
Slain be the atua that kills thee,
Begone behind, begone outside,
Begone to the stem, to the root of all things.
It is possessed, acquired.
Come forth to the world of being,
To the world of light,
The restored life.

A lament for his house

By Uamairangi

This house will stand
As once it was—
Spin on, spiders,
Build, you beetles—
You, of the tribe of Hakuturi,
Tribe of magic and madness,
Build this house as it was—
Every splinter, every chip—
There. It stands. It lives!
The fires of Tane burn within!
This tribe of the stump,
This tree cut short,
This broken people of the land
Will return from the ovens of the dead.
Tangaroa strikes from the sea,
The spear falls, blood runs
Over the hot stones of a feast
More terrible than the first,
Heaped high,
A return for the ovens of the dead.
Grant me power
Tane Mahuta of the forest
Cut deep,

Slash the sinew of Papatuanuku,
Thrust aside the barriers of Kupe,
Break the lashings of Uenuku's house.
Death take the thief.

Let this be a thought in the head
Of Ririwai.

How the trembling shakes me

By Pare-hokotoru. A chiefess seeks help to avenge herself for a tribal insult. Dogskin cloaks are symbolic of warfare.

How the trembling shakes me as the omen comes!
I am like a rock the tide beats upon, a rock of
    midnight delusion
That moves in the waves, the billows of the ocean!
It wearies me, but I am not angry.

Can the sun be brought down as he comes forth?
He hurries on throughout the day!

Let me enter the house of Werawera
That the dogskin cloak of Toka may be laid
    upon me!
You have kept it long enough! Let me have it, for I
    seek revenge!

My great longing now is for Te 'Paraha,
The man who alone appears on the moonless nights!

Oh! I am torn with fear

Composed by a woman who is the subject of gossip. Because of the death of her lover and the gossip, she believes she will die.

Oh! I am torn with fear,
Do not take me in your hand like a thief!
The tales lifted up over the groves at Te Tarua
Are all about me—they talk endlessly!
Clouds, farewell. Remain there alone.
I am gone with the descending current,
The sun disappearing at the river mouths at Kapenga,
To my lover dead of disease, for whom my heart cries
    out—
Oh he is here! He grasps me, comes close!

On the hilltops
Hilltops traditionally were places for melancholy feeling.

On the hilltops I visit the snares,
And my heart keeps surging.
Oh how can I quiet my heart,
That is tossed from north to south?

Love song

A woman is deserted by her husband. The clouds remind her of sorrow because they come from the district where he now lives. Line 6 addresses the clouds. Lines 7–8 address the husband.

Husband, it is well that you have left me.
There is nothing that comforts me now.
Who was it who turned away?
I am forgotten, and put aside.

I am consumed by the clouds flying hither.
You have come from my husband!
Why did you not in my youth
Release me when it first began?
Now the time comes for me to sit
Useless and unhappy. The sides of the canoe are
    shattered!

An ancient flute song

O shining cuckoo, cuckoo
with a long tail, calling
down to me your news
of the spring, come close!

The wind slams and pierces
loosed from Maunganui
where Ripiro lies under
and rituals are forgotten.

Let rituals be forgotten.
Rain on, O rain
tangled over the broad earth,
loom of the last darkness.

Come, cormorant at Te Taheke,
fly out of the wind-sleep inward,
make your nest here in the quiet
skies of the mind.

Sources

HAWAII

From "An ancient prayer": Abraham Fornander, *Fornander Collection of Hawaiian Antiquities and Folklore* (Bishop Museum Press, Honolulu, 1919), vol. 6, 509. Reprinted by permission of the publishers.

From "The Kumulipo": Martha Warren Beckwith, *The Kumulipo* (University of Chicago Press, Chicago, 1951), 58-60, 71-72, 73-74, 82-84, 87-88. Reprinted by permission of the publishers.

"The water of Kane": Nathaniel B. Emerson, *Unwritten Literature of Hawaii* (Bureau of American Ethnology, Washington, 1909), 258-259.

"An appeal for rain": Samuel Kamakau, *The Works of the People of Old (Na Hana a ka Po'e Kahiko)* (Bishop Museum Special Publication 51, Honolulu, 1976), 27. Reprinted by permission of the Bishop Museum Press.

"Prayer to Kane": David Malo, *Hawaiian Antiquities (Moolelo Hawaii)* (Bishop Museum Special Publication 2, 2nd ed., Honolulu, 1951), 158. Reprinted by permission of the Bishop Museum Press.

"Harvest prayer": Ibid., 158-159.

"House dedication prayer": E. S. Craighill Handy and Mary Kawena Pukui, *The Polynesian Family System in Ka-'u, Hawaii* (The Polynesian Society, Wellington, 1958), 113-114.

"Tree-felling song": Emerson, *Unwritten Literature,* 191.

Pele and Hi'i-aka

"The coming of Pele": Mary Kawena Pukui and Alfons Korn, *The Echo of Our Song* (University Press of Hawaii, Honolulu, 1973), 54-55. Reprinted by permission of the University of Hawaii Press.

"The spy": based on translation of Nathaniel B. Emerson, *Pele and Hi'i-aka* (Honolulu, 1915), 31.

"Watch your way": Ibid., 31.

"Songs of the girl without hands": Ibid., 70-71.

Sources

"Stormy weather": Ibid., 90-91.
"Kauhi": Ibid., 93.
"Hi'i-aka's song at Ka-'ena": Pukui and Korn, *Echo of Our Song*, 66-67.
"Hi'i-aka's song for the Stone of Kaua'i": Ibid., 71.
"Songs to the ghost of Lohi'au": based on translation of Emerson, *Pele and Hi'i-aka*, 132-133.
"Hi'i-aka chants to restore Lohi'au to life": Ibid., 147.
"Vision of the burning": Ibid., 186.
"A storm, a rough surf": Ibid., 203-204.
"The fires of Pele": Ibid., 211.
"Lohi'au's song": Ibid., 238.
From "Fallen is the chief": Fornander, *Hawaiian Antiquities and Folklore*, vol. 6, 373-375.
From "A chant for the island of Maui": Samuel Kamakau, *Ruling Chiefs of Hawaii* (Kamehameha Schools Press, Honolulu, 1961), 114-115. Reprinted by permission of the publishers.
"A kapu is placed": Fornander, *Hawaiian Antiquities and Folklore*, vol. 5, 248.
"Love song": Emerson, *Unwritten Literature*, 76.
"The salt pond of Mana": Abraham Fornander, *An Account of the Polynesian Race* (Trübner and Co., London, 1878-1885), vol. 2, 357-358.
From "Ka-'ahu-manu's dirge for Ke'e-au-moku": Kamakau, *Ruling Chiefs*, 317.
From "Birth chant for Kau-i-ke-ao-uli": Pukui and Korn, *Echo of Our Song*, 20-22.
"A name song for Princess Nahi'ena'ena": Emerson, *Unwritten Literature*, 209.
"Song": Ibid., 211.
"Shark song": Ibid., 222.
"Chant composed while drunk": John Papa Ii, *Fragments of Hawaiian History* (Bishop Museum Press, Honolulu, 1959), 108. Reprinted by permission of the publishers.
"Lament on the death of a first child": Handy and Pukui, *Polynesian Family System*, 155-156.
From "A name chant for Kupake'e": Ibid., 85.
"Song of the chanter Ka-'ehu": Pukui and Korn, *Echo of Our Song*, 128-129.
"Piano at evening": Ibid., 107-108.

Sources   211

SAMOA

"From a creation chant": Adapted from Margaret Mead, *Social Organization of Manu'a* (Bishop Museum Bulletin 76, Honolulu, 1930; 2nd. ed., 1969), 152–153. Reprinted by permission of the Bishop Museum Press.

"Chant for the whale": S. Locke, "The Visit of Pou to Hawaiki to Procure the Kumara," *Journal of the Polynesian Society* 30, 1921, 40–41.

"Lovers' farewell": O. P. Nelson, "Legends of Samoa," *Journal of the Polynesian Society* 34, 1925, 133.

TONGA

"The weather shore of Vavau": Katharine Luomala, *Voices on the Wind* (Bishop Museum Press, Honolulu, 1955), 32–33. Reprinted by permission of the publishers. I have rephrased some of this version. See also William Mariner, *An Account of the Natives of the Tongan Islands,* ed. John Martin, vol. 2 (London, 1871), 333, 402–405.

"Love song": E. E. V. Collocott, *Tales and Poems of Tonga* (Bishop Museum Bulletin 46, Honolulu, 1928), 126. Reprinted by permission of the Bishop Museum Press.

"How I love her way": Ibid., 89.

"Poem of Falepapalangi to Mamaeaepoto": Ibid., 72–73.

"Poem of Veehala": Ibid., 107.

THE SOCIETY ISLANDS

"Creation chant": Fornander, *An Account of the Polynesian Race,* vol. 1, 221–223.

"Chant for a royal birth": Teuira Henry, *Ancient Tahiti* (Bishop Museum Bulletin 48, Honolulu, 1928), 183. Reprinted by permission of the Bishop Museum Press.

"Anointing the royal child": Ibid., 183.

"Chant to usher in the dawn": Ibid., 165.

"The song of Ru's sister": Ibid., 460.

"Warrior's taunting song": Ibid., 305.

"Song of Pa'ea": Ibid., 79.

"Invocation for fire-walking": adapted from J. L. Young, "The Umu-ti Ceremonial Fire Walking as Practiced in the Eastern Pacific," *Journal of the Polynesian Society* 34, 1925, 215.

"A chief's refusal": Henry Adams, *Tahiti* (Scholars Facsimiles and Reprints, New York, 1947), 25.
"A chief's lament for home": Ibid., 35.

THE TUAMOTUS

"Creation chant": Kenneth Emory, "The Tahitian Account of Creation by Mare," *Journal of the Polynesian Society* 47, 1938, 50. Reprinted by permission of Kenneth Emory and The Polynesian Society.
"Greeting of Tane": Kenneth Emory, "Tuamotuan Concepts of Creation," *Journal of the Polynesian Society* 49, 1940, 94. Reprinted by permission of Kenneth Emory and The Polynesian Society.
"Farewell to my land": Henry, *Ancient Tahiti*, 502.
"Rata's lament for his father": J. F. Stimson, *Tuamotuan Legends of the Demigods* (Bishop Museum Bulletin 148, Honolulu, 1937), 137. Reprinted by permission of the Bishop Museum Press.
"Chant to announce a catch of turtle": Kenneth Emory, *Tuamotuan Religious Structures and Ceremonies* (Bishop Museum Bulletin 191, Honolulu, 1947), 60–61. Reprinted by permission of the Bishop Museum Press.
"Prayer offering turtle flesh to the gods": Ibid., 76.
"Prayer for the arrival of turtle at the temple": Ibid., 69.
"Chant for Horahora": J. F. Stimson, *The Legends of Maui and Tahaki* (Bishop Museum Bulletin 127, Honolulu, 1934), 61–62. Reprinted by permission of the Bishop Museum Press.
"Chant of Kororupo": J. F. Stimson, *Tuamotuan Religion* (Bishop Museum Bulletin 103, Honolulu, 1933), 43. Reprinted by permission of the Bishop Museum Press.

THE MARQUESAS

"Chant honoring a first-born son": E. S. Craighill Handy and Jane Lothrop Winne, *Music in the Marquesas Islands* (Bishop Museum Bulletin 17, Honolulu, 1925), 41. Reprinted by permission of the Bishop Museum Press.
"Love song": Samuel H. Elbert, "Chants and Love Songs of the Marquesas Islands, French Oceania," *Journal of the Polynesian Society* 50, 1941, 76–77. Reprinted by permission of Samuel H. Elbert and The Polynesian Society.

Sources

"Be careful": Ibid., 81-82.
"Hiva'oa balances": Ibid., 82-83.
"The faufe'e bird": Ibid., 83-84.
"Strong fires disturb": Ibid., 85-86.
"When a man's body is young": Ibid., 87-88.

EASTER ISLAND

"A chant of creation": Adapted by Antony Alpers from Alfred Metraux, *Ethnology of Easter Island* (Bishop Museum Bulletin 160, Honolulu, 1940), 320-322. Reprinted by permission of the Bishop Museum Press.
"A prayer for rain": Metraux, *Ethnology of Easter Island,* 330.
"Dampened by dew": Ibid., 356.
"Love song": Ibid., 356.
"You are sick with love": Ibid., 357.
"O Manu": Ibid., 357.

MANGAREVA

"Tahaki's Drum": Te Rangi Hiroa (Peter H. Buck), *Ethnology of Mangareva* (Bishop Museum Bulletin 157, Honolulu, 1938), 322-323. Reprinted by permission of the Bishop Museum Press.
"Song of departure": Ibid., 324.
"The message of the frigate bird": Ibid., 330-331.
"The rich and the poor": Ibid., 342-343.
"The flower at the spring": Ibid., 349.
"Joy turns to sadness": Ibid., 350.
"Sea burial of Toga's daughter": Ibid., 356.
"The sacred house": Ibid., 360.
"The casting out of love": Ibid., 365.
"I am left alone": Ibid., 372-373.
"Lament": Ibid., 373-374.
"The canoe of Mamau-ora": Ibid., 381.
"Haul away": Ibid., 388-389.
"Song of things in the upper world": Ibid., 375.
"Lament for old age": Ibid., 390-391.

COOK ISLANDS

"Prayer over a human sacrifice to Rongo": William Wyatt Gill, *Myths and Songs from the South Pacific* (Henry S. King and Co., London, 1876), 295-296.

"Where has she gone": Ibid., 179–180.
"Puvai leading a band of ghosts to the underworld": Ibid., 199–202.
"Death lament for Varenga": Ibid., 208–210.

TUVALU

"Vaitupu songs": D. G. Kennedy, *Field notes on the Culture of Vaitupu, Ellice Islands* (Avery, New Zealand, 1931), 128, 131.

KAPINGAMARANGI

"The post standing in the sky": Kenneth Emory, *Kapingamarangi: Social and Religious Life of a Polynesian Atoll* (Bishop Museum Bulletin 228, Honolulu, 1965), 240. Reprinted by permission of the Bishop Museum Press.
"Love song": Ibid., 172–173.
"I go down to the lagoon": Ibid., 36.
"I am on the water": Ibid., 188–189.
"Chant for the bonito canoe": Ibid., 216.
"Search for": Ibid., 241.
"The man stayed": Ibid., 241.

TIKOPIA

"Lament for a friend": Raymond Firth, *Tikopia Ritual and Belief* (Beacon Paperback, Boston, 1968), 113. Reprinted by permission of George Allen & Unwin.
"Dream song": Ibid., 361.

NEW ZEALAND

"Creation chant": Johannes C. Andersen, *Myths and Legends of the Polynesians* (Harrap and Co., London, 1928), 353.
"Creation chant": John White, *The Ancient History of the Maori* (George Didsbury, Wellington, 1887–1890), vol. 2, 107.
"Creation chant": Richard Taylor, *Te Ika a Maui or New Zealand and Its Inhabitants* (Wertheim and Macintosh, London, 1855), 14–15.
"The creation of woman": Barry M. Mitcalfe, *Poetry of the Maori* (Paul's Book Arcade, Hamilton, 1961), 41–42.
'Chant for bailing a canoe": Percy S. Smith, "The Aotea Canoe," *Journal of the Polynesian Society,* 1900, 224.

"Arrival at New Zealand": Arthur S. Thomson, *The Story of New Zealand* (J. Murray, London, 1859), 61.
"From a lament for a son who burned to death": Leslie G. Kelly, *Tainui, The History of Hoturoa and His Descendants* (The Polynesian Society, Wellington, 1949), 264-266.
"Prayer for victory in battle": Percy S. Smith, "Wars of Northern Against Southern Tribes of New Zealand," *Journal of the Polynesian Society*, 1899, 158-159.
"Chant to incite warriors": Andersen, *Myths and Legends*, 181.
"A war chant": James Cowan, *The Maori Yesterday and Today* (Whitcombe and Tombs, Auckland, 1930), 102.
"Spiders, hide my face": Ibid., 231.
"Te Rauparaha's farewell to Kawhia": Pei Te Hurinui Jones, *King Potatau* (The Polynesian Society, Wellington, 1959), 84-85.
"Potatau's song of sorrow": Ibid., 208-209.
"Dirge for a chief": Peter Buck, *Vikings of the Sunrise* (Lippincott, New York, 1938), 282-283. Reprinted by permission of Harper & Row.
"A ritual spell": Barry Mitcalfe, *Maori Poetry, The Singing Word* (Victoria University Press, Wellington, 1974), 28. Reprinted by permission of Price Milburn.
"Vision": Ibid., 82.
"Song of mourning": Ibid., 49-50.
"A charm: Is it the Wind?": Ibid., 36-37.
"Song of a second wife": Ibid., 54-55.
"The deserted girl's lament": Cowan, *The Maori*, 95.
"A mourning song for Rangiahao": Mitcalfe, *Maori Poetry*, 65.
"A song of sickness": Ibid., 64.
"Chant to restore breath to a dead person": Elsdon Best, "Spiritual Concepts of the Maori," *Journal of the Polynesian Society*, 1901, 10.
"A lament for his house": Mitcalfe, *Maori Poetry*, 38.
"How the trembling shakes me": Margaret Orbell, *Maori Poetry* (Heinemann Educational Books, Auckland, 1978), 27. Reprinted by permission of the publishers.
"Oh! I am torn with fear": Ibid., 23.
"On the hilltops": Ibid., 13.
"Love song": Mervyn McLean and Margaret Orbell, *Traditional Songs of the Maori* (A. H. & A. W. Reed, Wellington,

1975), 268. Reprinted by permission of Auckland University Press.

"An ancient flute song": Allen Curnow, *The Penguin Book of New Zealand Verse* (Penguin, London, 1960), 84. Reprinted by permission of Allen Curnow and Roger Oppenheim.

Every effort has been made to trace copyright holders to whom proper acknowledgment is due.